OH! CALCUTTA! *premièred at the Eden Theatre in New York City on June 17, 1969, after thirty-nine preview performances. It was produced by Hillard Elkins in association with Michael White and Gordon Crowe, and was an E.P.I.C. Production. Music and lyrics were by The Open Window; choreography by Margo Sappington; sets by James Tilton; lighting by David Segal; costumes by Fred Voelpel; projected media designed by Gardner Compton and Emile Ardolino; production supervisor, Michael Thoma; associate producer, George Platt. It was devised by Kenneth Tynan and conceived and directed by Jacques Levy, with the following cast:*

Raina Barrett, Mark Dempsey, Katie Drew-Wilkinson, Boni Enten, Bill Macy, Alan Rachins, Leon Russom, Margo Sappington, Nancy Tribush, George Welbes, and The Open Window (Robert Dennis, Peter Schickele, and Stanley Walden.)

Photographs from the New York production are by Friedman-Abeles.

❦ *An entertainment with music devised by Kenneth Tynan*
directed by Jacques Levy
Grove Press, Inc., New York

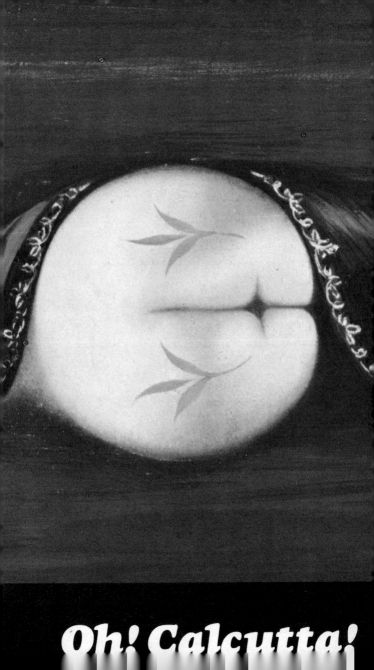

Oh! Calcutta!

Library of Congress Catalog Card
Number 78-82940
First Printing
Design is by Stephanie Tevonian
Editorial Supervision: Bill Liberman
Manufactured in the United States
of America

Contributors

Julian Barry
Samuel Beckett
Jules Feiffer
Dan Greenburg
John Lennon
Jacques Levy
Pat McCormick
Leonard Melfi
David Newman and
   Robert Benton
Edna O'Brien
The Open Window
Sam Shepard
Kenneth Tynan
Sherman Yellen

Contents

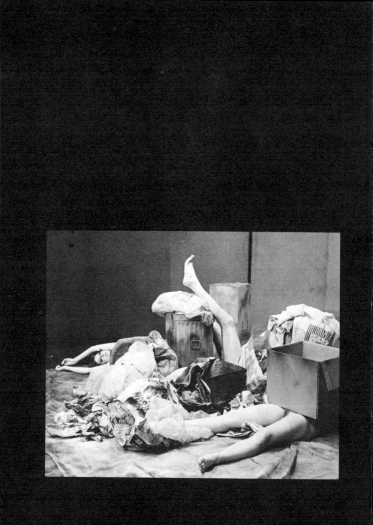

ℰ *Prologue*

CURTAIN

1. Faint light on stage littered with miscellaneous rubbish, including naked people. Hold about five seconds.

2. Faint brief cry and immediately inspiration and slow increase of light together reaching maximum together in about ten seconds. Silence and hold about five seconds.

3. Expiration and slow decrease of light together reaching minimum together (light as in 1) in about ten seconds and immediately cry as before. Silence and hold about five seconds.

CURTAIN

RUBBISH No verticals, all scattered and lying.

CRY Instant of recorded vagitus. Important that two cries be identical, switching on and off strictly synchronized light and breath.

BREATH Amplified recording.

MAXIMUM LIGHT Not bright. If $0 =$ dark and $10 =$ bright, light should move from about 3 to 6 and back.

—*Samuel Beckett*

Taking Off the Robe

Introductory music is playing. The actors enter up-stage in semi-darkness, dressed in their own street clothes (whatever they happen to be wearing.)

White robes, each with "Oh! Calcutta!" written on the back, come into place hanging on the upstage wall. The actors, facing away from the audience, undress informally and quickly, chatting with each other and changing into the robes. A group of workers dressing for their jobs. Their street clothes disappear. Now the actors in their "team uniforms" are left on a bare stage. They move down front in a line across the stage —each one in a different colored light. (Note: This is the only time in the evening that the skin of the actors is colored anything but normal. No projections on the bodies, no play of lights on the bodies will take place at any other time during the "entertainment." Except in this number, bodies are to be flesh and only flesh at all times.)

Now the song "Oh! Calcutta!" begins, as a white spot-light picks out the actor furthest stage right and he be-gins to take off his robe. Films and slides of him play all around the stage, introducing him. In this first sec-tion, all the actors are stripping, but none of them completes the act. They are going through a "routine" —not selling, a little bit tough, take it or leave it. It gets to a certain point, stops, repeats from the begin-ning—each actor being spotlighted in turn across the

11

stage and introduced with films and slides.

*When all are introduced, they become a frieze in col-
ored lights. Then the process begins again from right to
left—this time no spotlight as each actor completes the
action of stripping, holding the robe over his shoulders,
and facing front in a neutral attitude. After the last
one is finished, white light comes on as they all freeze.
They stand there, looking at the audience, naked.*

*Then they back away upstage, holding up the robes in
front so that they are hidden as lights dim and films
play on the white robes. The actors weave in and out
—side to side—making the film "screen" move. And
finally, they move quickly out of the way to one side,
while the film continues on the walls.*

*Then, in a line, they move across the stage, singing
"Oh! Calcutta!"They turn and slowly march upstage,
proud as bullfighters, and exit where they had come
from.*

Music has built to a crescendo, and ends.

BLACKOUT

❦ Dick and Jane

Night in a bedroom. Lights are out.
The stage is black.

JANE: Not that way—(*Grunts uncomfortably.*)

DICK (*grunts uncomfortably*): Ouch!

JANE: I'm over here. (DICK *grunts uncomfortably.*)
Wait a minute. (*Grunts.*)

DICK: Will you stop? (JANE *grunts uncomfortably.*)
Why can't we do it—

JANE: Now where did you go? (DICK *grunts uncomfortably.*) There. There. Perfect. Now! Now!

Pause.

DICK: Shit.

JANE: If you'd listen to me—

DICK: Hold it.

JANE: You're moving all wrong.

DICK: Why can't we do it—

JANE: Don't be in such a hurry. I'm not going anywhere. Let me do that. (*Pause.*) See? I told you to let me—

DICK: Shit.

JANE: I'm over here.

DICK: Hold it—

JANE: That's better. (*Pause.* DICK *makes a series of grunts.*) You're going too fast. (DICK *makes slower grunts.*) Faster. (DICK *makes faster grunts.*) Oh—ohh—ohhhhhhhh—

17

He pants, out of breath, as she sighs happily. A period of silence. Lights go on to reveal a bed, nearly stage size, with a mattress constructed of oak-stained wooden planks. A strobe is clamped to the headboard. JANE, *naked, lies under a sheet that doesn't quite cover the bed.* DICK, *his back to us, is sitting at far edge of bed. He is fully dressed in a business suit and is putting on his hat.*

DICK: I have an appointment.

JANE: You have a what?! At four in the morning you have a *what?!*

DICK: I have an 8:30 appointment. Have to get cross-town, shower and shave. Change suits. Eat breakfast. (*Checks his watch.*) Really, it was great. (*Starts toward the door.*) It was the best.

JANE: You bastard!

DICK: (*returns and sits, very formally, at edge of bed*): What can I tell you? It was great. (*Stiffly takes her hand.*) You're the greatest ever. (*Dispassionately takes her in his arms.*) It's you and me all the way, kid.

Both pose lifelessly, then she begins to respond. She pulls him down on top of her, takes off his hat, switches off light. Pause.

JANE: Where are you?

Door opens. Light from hall illuminates DICK *at door, hat on, fully dressed.*

DICK: The greatest. (*He exits.*)

Silence.

JANE (*very quiet*): Bastard. (*Long pause. She shouts:*) You bastard!

DICK *enters, crosses to* JANE'S *bed, leaving door ajar, so that for a while it remains the only source of illumination.*

DICK (*sits on edge of bed*): I'll be honest with you. I'm not getting as much out of this as I expected. You know what I mean, it's not working out, it's nobody's fault, we've had some laughs, what the hell, right?

She stares at him silently. He is increasingly uneasy.

You're a bitch, you know that? An aggressive man-eating bitch! Move this way—that way—too fast—too slow—up—down—stop—start—You goddamn traffic cop! Police brutality—that's what you're guilty of! A maid. I'm nothing but a maid. I come in three times a week, make up your body, and go home.

JANE: Rush home.

DICK: Why not? It's quitting time, isn't it? After I boff you, my time is my own.

JANE: To spend on more exotic pleasures.

DICK: I do what I do the best way I know how to do it, then I go home and enjoy myself.

JANE: And I know how.

DICK: Big deal.

JANE: With your filthy pornography.

DICK: It beats the clean-cut pornography I get around here.

JANE: I'm sorry I can't rise to the level of your fantasy life.

DICK: You could if you wanted to.

JANE: Don't degrade me.

DICK: You're not degraded in my fantasies, you're honored. I honor you.

JANE (*shocked*): You don't use me in your fantasies— (*He smiles.*) You bastard! I'll sue you!

DICK: When you're not in charge you get very uptight.

JANE: You have no right!

DICK: Now you want to police my fantasies.

JANE: It's my person! I should have some rights about the role I play. What's wrong with doing it the regular way?

DICK: My father and mother did it the regular way.

JANE: You're jaded.

DICK: You're dead. I thought you liked to talk afterwards. All right, we're talking. Except that's not enough, is it? If I give in to you on talking the next

19

request is to pet you. Except both of us pet you because you're guiding my hand: higher, lower, over here, over there. Baby, I just like to get laid. And when I have the temerity to suggest a simple little experiment—

JANE: You're sick.

DICK: If it gives me pleasure, you tell me it's sick. To you anything more exotic than this way, that way is a perversion. Screwing you is like screwing a cookie cutter!

JANE: There's still such a thing as morality!

DICK: Morality? We're not talking about Vietnam! You want to know why I get the hell out of here as fast as I can? Because of tension. This is a very tense bed.

JANE: Not because of me!

DICK: Sure. You're free.

JANE: I *am* free! (*She stares at him in silent challenge.*)

DICK (*starts toward the door*): O.K. I'll get my equipment.

JANE: No!

DICK: She's free. What's the point? You don't like fucking unless you're talking. You fuck for companionship. I'm a good fucker but a lousy companion. We're incompatible.

JANE: I can't be what I'm not.

DICK: You can't be what you are. I'm trying to free you. (DICK *reaches for her. She recoils.*) See how tense you are? (*Puts hand on her neck.*) It's a steel column. I could break rocks on it. Here, let me show you a little exercise (*Stands on his head.*) Try it. (*She hesitates.*) Come on, try it. It'll relax you.

JANE: What will you be doing?

DICK: Come on, you're making me mad!

JANE: I don't trust you.

DICK (*shouts*): Do we have to fight when I'm standing on my goddamn head? I didn't think it was possible, but you make me tense even this way!

JANE, *with great awkwardness, tries a headstand.* DICK *finally rights himself, puts his arms around her legs and holds her in upside-down position.*

Doesn't that feel great?

JANE: Let me down!

DICK *starts to force his head between her legs.*

Let me down, you sick bastard! Help! Rape!

He drops her legs.

DICK: Some people can't handle freedom. You're one of them. I banish you to permanent slavery. (*He starts to leave.*)

JANE: Help me!

DICK: I can only help those who help themselves.

JANE: That's *God,* you idiot! What are you doing?

He is taking off his clothes.

Dick, I warn you—

He walks toward her. She screams. He passes her and crosses to bed. He picks up her dress, sniffs at it, puts it over his head, then starts to get into it.

You maniac!

She lunges for dress. He turns away from her, throws her his suit.

DICK: Role reversal time!

She drops suit.

Don't crush it! Dammit, put it on! It'll set you free!

JANE (*picks up suit, rips jacket*): You want me to be free? (*Rips sleeve off.*) All right, I'm free! (*Rips other sleeve.*) Free! (*Rips trousers.*) Free!

JANE *throws herself on floor, goes through epileptic-like contortions.* DICK *watches, electrified.*

DICK: You've got it!

JANE (*thrashing*): I'm free! I'm free! I'm free! I'm free!

DICK (*starts off*): I'll be right back. Stay that way. Don't change! (*Exits.*)

JANE: Free!

DICK *enters wearing mask, carrying whip in one hand, black leather, high-heeled, laced boots in the other. He throws them on bed, exits running. A basketball bounces in. He enters wheeling bicycle,*

carrying riding crop and watermelon. Basket on bike is filled with paint cans. He parks bike, reads labels on cans.

DICK: Purple. Emerald Green. Day-glo Orange. (*To* JANE, *who has slowly stopped thrashing and has risen to her knees in order to see better*:) You'll see, this is going to be great! (*He tosses paint can and brush at her.*) Start with this. Day-glo looks great on boobs. Be free!

Dashes out. Colored balloons float in. He re-enters,

carrying large tin tub. Inside the tub sprawls enormous female store-window dummy.

Snap it up! Can't you get those cans open?

DICK *exits. Re-enters carrying phonograph and movie projector. Turns them on: deafeningly loud rock, accompanied by a light show. Light show intensifies, becomes blinding. The last action we see is* DICK *leaping through air at* JANE, *an open umbrella in his hand. After a suitable lapse of time the rock record ends, the light show goes off, the room is black.*

O boy, O boy, O boy, O boy, O boy. Did you ever dream it could be that good? I've never had it that good. Have you, Jane? The best I ever had it. You know, it's crazy, but I feel so close to you, as if for the first time I've seen you—I've seen your soul. And you've seen my soul, Jane. What does good or bad or ugly or sick mean when we've seen each other's souls? Listen to me talk. I never talk this way. Would you believe it's me, Jane? Christ, we've got so much to talk about. (*He lights a match.*) Jane. Where are you, Jane?

Match provides enough illumination for him to be seen crawling out from under overturned tub. He finds the lamp somewhere on the floor and turns it on. The room is a shambles, debris everywhere, the bed is broken.

Jane! (*He starts going through debris.*) Hey, Jane! (*Looks under tub.*) Where are you? (*Looks under bed, goes through blankets.*) Jane! Hey, Jane! Hey, weren't you here? Don't tell me you missed it! Jane! Jane! (*Opens door.*) Jane! (*Exits, his voice fading as he disappears down the hall.*) Jane! You should've been there! Jane! (*His voice dies.*)

Lights fade.

END

Suite for Five Letters

Five players, dressed in formal attire, are seated on high stools, in concert style. They sing with serious purity of tone and a limpid nostalgic sweetness, their thoughts often overlapping slightly.

MAN 2:   Letters to the editor: London, 1939—New York, 1969. Authors unknown.

GIRL 1:   Dear Editor. . .
      I had my first real corset
      At twelve years of age.
      It fitted my babyish measurements
      Closely.
      My mother insisted my waist should be kept at that size
      And never allowed to enlarge,
      Though my bust and my hips were permitted to do so.

GIRL 2:   Dear Editor. . .
      I have read with much interest
      The letters on the subject of punishing daughters;
      Many of your readers feel that girls should be chastised,
      Even when in their teens. . .
      Chastised. . .

MAN 1: Dear Editor. . .
I believe it can be truthfully said that most men enjoy seeing girls wear high heels.

GIRL 1: When I was married, I reduced my waist to fifteen inches on special occasions.
I shall never forget walking sedately across the lawns at Brighton on a Sunday morning. . .

GIRL 2: Until we were fourteen,
The only punishment my sister and I received
Were ordinary spankings, draped across our mother's knee.
After that age, we were soundly whipped.
. . . Whipped. . .

MAN 2: Dear Editor. . .
I'm rather keen on unusual kinds of adornment.
Such as curious earrings,
Nose ornaments,
Mackintosh capes, and
Starched petticoats. . .
Starched petticoats. . .

GIRL 3: Dear Editor. . .

Here is the latest news
About my attempts
At making my own rubber wear.
One of your readers,
"Waterproof Winnie,"
Suggested rayon Directoire knickers, which I
    wear
With the rubber next to my skin.

MAN 1: There are many reasons why high heels are attractive.

MAN 2: The other day I saw a lady wearing wide octagonal platinum rings.

MAN 1: One is the exquisite beauty of the shoes themselves.

MAN 2: Right through the lobes of her ears.

GIRL 1: Once I met an old school-fellow whose waist had been laced to the same size as mine.

GIRL 2: We received on our bare bottoms up to a dozen strokes with a long thin cane.

GIRL 1: How we laughed at the scenes we had caused.

27

MAN 2: Rather peculiar piercings. I wonder how this was done.

MAN 1: High heels cause a marked accentuation of the swelling curve of the instep.

MAN 2: If any reader can explain, I shall be pleased.

GIRL 3: My rubber knickers fit tightly 'round hips and waist.
The resultant appearance is very chic.

GIRL 2: My husband says I'm an ideal wife,
And attributes it
To the kind but firm
Way in which I was brought up.

MAN 2: Other readers must have seen unusual piercings like the ones I have described.

GIRL 1: Fifteen-inch waists, of course, were only for special occasions.

GIRL 3: I am never allowed to forget what I'm wearing—

MAN 1: From six to nine inches high—

GIRL 2: Of an errant wife or daughter—

MAN 1: In shiny patent leather—

In a capella *chorus*:

GIRL 1: Yours truly. . .

MAN 1: Yours truly. . .

GIRL 2: Yours truly. . .

MAN 2: Yours truly. . .

GIRL 3: Yours truly. . .

This phrase becomes a climax, in which for the first time all are singing harmoniously in unison. Then each withdraws into isolation again.

MAN 1: "Shoe Shop Susie" (*Repeated through the following:*)

GIRL 1: "Wasp-Waisted Widow" (*Repeated through the following:*)

GIRL 2: "Happy, happy, happy, happy, happy Wife" (*Repeated through the following:*)

MAN 2: "Observant Reader" (*Repeated through the following:*)

GIRL 3: "Lover of Rubber."

The musical tone changes to a modern rock beat. As it reaches a higher intensity. . .

MAN 2: Dear Editor:
Nice guy, fifty—civilized, generous,
White, unprejudiced, not handicapped,
Wishes to meet limb-deficient woman
For exploration of mutual interest.
Sincere, Lonely Male.

GIRL 3: Dear Editor:
Dancer and actress,
35-23-36,
Any pose you desire.
Love a little or a lot.
Will do exotic dancing—
And also a little acting—
Sexy Swiss Miss.

GIRL 1: Dear Editor:
Seeking males and females
To serve as my slaves.
Get down on your knees
And write me now.
Strong Dominant Mistress.

29

MAN 1: Dear Editor:
I know your male dog's needs.
I'll service all their animal desires.
I'm well-equipped to handle everything.
Your dog will be so satisfied.
Canine Swinger.

GIRL 2 (*out of "Happy, happy, happy, happy, happy"*):
Wife with nympho-like tendencies
Seeking rugged, virile-type male
Who went to the head of his French class.
Serious Slave.

The music slowly fades. Pause. The players relax. Slowly, GIRL 1 lifts her gown and places one hand between her legs, simulating masturbation. She begins what will become the personal sexual fantasies of the moment for each of the players on stage. The actors remain neutral, keeping their minds a blank until it is their moment to start speaking. Then, whatever actual sexual fantasy pops into their mind is spoken aloud, no holds barred. It is very important to this piece that the fantasies of the actors be fresh improvisations each performance so that they can be taken by the fantasies rather than being in control of lines they have come to learn. Sometimes the fantasies may be funny but that should not be their sole intent and the language used should be blunt and to the point. The fantasies are spoken to a light musical vamp as each player's fantasy becomes dominant, then subordinate, until all fantasies reach a dominant position at once and fade out to nothingness as the lights dim to black.

END

🎵 Will Answer All Sincere Replies

As the scene shifts there is a song:

> I'll write to you
> Ev'ry day.
> (I'll write to you once ev'ry day.)
> Please listen to
> What I say.
> (Please listen to what I say.)
> Sincere replies is all I want
> To see me through.
> Sincere replies is all I need
> Till I see you.

VOICE: *"KANSAS AREA—Swinging couple. He 31, she 28, attractive, Caucasian. Seek similar minded couple for fun, parties. Interested in French and Greek culture. Discretion assured. No prudes please. Photo a must. Will answer all sincere replies. KANS 7-385b-X."*

Lights up on living room of DALE *and* SUE ELLEN WALKER; *middle-income housing development type home in suburbs of Kansas City. Furniture and decor are typical and bad: nothing white anywhere, all "pastels" in scratchy fabrics on chairs, sofas, etc. Three matching clown paintings on the walls, and a studio portrait of a little girl, their daughter: a photograph which has been "tinted in oils." Mosaic coffee table, big fake Italian provincial stereo cabi-*

*net, aqua carpeting and so on. There is one couch,
two chairs, coffee table "conversation area" at right.
Another couch, facing away from audience, upstage.
Front door left, door leading to bedroom right, another door to kitchen upstage right. Little bowls and
trays on every end table, coffee table, and flat surface
in the room.*

As lights come up, SUE ELLEN *is talking on the phone.
Twenty-eight, pretty, she wears a pair of hostess
pyjamas that could only have been bought in Kansas City. Making two stiff drinks at the formica bar
is* DALE, *thirty-one, tall, round-faced, and friendly-
looking, with a short brush cut. He is nervous, drinking to calm himself. He wears a cardigan and sports
shirt.*

SUE ELLEN: Hi, Sis, how's everythin'? . . . Debbie's not
givin' you too much trouble now, is she? . . . Good.
But if she gives you any sass, you just swat her one
and tell her I said so. . . Did she eat all her dinner
up? . . . Well, you know how she is about spaghetti.
Dale says she's gonna turn *into* spaghetti one of these
days, she loves it so much. . . Listen now, don't let
her watch T.V. after 8:30. . . . Okay, Sis. You're an
angel to do this, I mean it. . . Well, by the time we
drive back from Elmwood it'll be so late, I just don't
know. . . I'll pick her up around ten in the mornin',
O. K.? . . . Night-night, Sis. (*Hangs up phone.*)

DALE (*his way of covering up is to deny his fear and
nervousness by pretending the feelings are* SUE
ELLEN'S): You know, there's not a thing for you to
be nervous about.

SUE ELLEN: Dale, I feel funny. That's the truth of it. I
do agree our sex life was in need of a good shaking
up last year, but then we started that pretending stuff
—me going to the Double D Show Girl Lounge and
playing a call girl and you coming in pretending you
were a salesman—And registering at that motel, and
that funny look the bellboy gave us. Now that was
good, wasn't it—and darn sexy—

DALE: Honey, this is the age of the sex revolution—
It's the wave of the future—nothin' for you to be
nervous about. Look now, folks who could write a
letter like that, why they're just the same as us.
(*Pausing, choosing the word.*) Style-setters.

SUE ELLEN: Dale, let's not talk about it. (*Looking
around.*) Where are the ice cubes?

DALE (*won't shut up*): The way I see it, there's a
new feelin' of . . . freedom that just brings us closer
closer together, Sue Ellen. It's I mean. . . it's a way
of really trusting one anoth—. . . .

SUE ELLEN (*tense*): Dale, I said I'd do it and here I
am *goin'* to do it, but I am just fed up to *here* with
talking about it. (*Handing him a bag.*) Now put
some Fritos in the lazy Susan.

Suddenly the doorbell rings. They freeze, terrified.

DALE (*suddenly throwing all the responsibility to her*):
You *sure* you want to go through with this? (*She
gives him an outraged WHAT???!! reaction as he
goes to the door.*) Remember. Don't tell 'em where
I work!

*He opens the front door. Enter MONTE JACKSON JR.
and his wife, CHERIE. They are both in their 40's, and
it is obvious from their clothes that they are from a
lower income bracket. He wears a zip-up windbreaker
and his left arm is in a cast and sling; in addition, all
the fingers of his left hand appear to have been
broken, since they are wired to a circular splint attached to the cast. In short, they are not, at first
glance, what the WALKERS have been hoping for.*

MONTE: Is this the Walker residence?

DALE: Yes, anything I can do for you?

MONTE: (*loudly*): Hiya, buddy! How they hangin'?

DALE: Um . . . uh . . . are you . . . uh . . . Mr. Jackson?

MONTE: Affirmative!

CHERIE: Hi, honey, I'm Cherie. (*Putting the accent on
the last syllable of her name. She carries an airline
bag.*)

MONTE (*coming on as if he owned the place*): Brother,

am I glad we found this place! We rang damn near every doorbell on the block lookin' for you folks.

SUE ELLEN *looks ready to faint at this news. They are now in the living room.* CHERIE *removes her raincoat.*

CHERIE (*suddenly aware they are both staring at her blouse*): See somethin' you like?

DALE: Huh?

MONTE (*to them*): Some set, huh? Wait'll you see 'em in action. (*Paying no attention to the* WALKERS' *stunned silence, he walks familiarly to* SUE ELLEN.) No offense, missus. You're no slouch in the knockers department yourself.

SUE ELLEN (*bolting from the spot; she takes the coats and crosses. Then, sotto voce*): Sex revolution, wave of the future, eh?

DALE (*goes to bar, where five bottles of ready-mix cocktail bottles await*): You folks want a drink? We've got Old-Fashioneds, Martinis, Side Cars, Manhattans—

MONTE (*sitting down on couch*): Got any Schlitz?

DALE: Uh . . . no.

MONTE (*jocularly*): When you're outta Schlitz, you're outta beer.

CHERIE *laughs appreciatively.*

DALE: I think I have a bottle of Budweiser here someplace.

MONTE (*fine with him*): That Bud, that's beer! (*Laughs again.*)

SUE ELLEN (*still trying to play gracious hostess to* CHERIE): Would you like a drink, Mrs. Jackson?

CHERIE: Cher*ie*, honey. (*Lets that sink in.*) I'll take a Fresca if you've got one. . . . Lovely place you've got here. (*Pause.*)

SUE ELLEN (*this has been bothering her; now she blurts it out*): Say . . . was that really you in the photos?

MONTE (*with offended dignity*): We never send phonies.

SUE ELLEN: Well . . . well, you just look . . . different, I guess.

MONTE: You put a little on in the keester since then, you know it?

CHERIE (*the coquette*): ME! (*To* DALE *and* SUE ELLEN:) He's always bad-mouthin' my butt, this goon.

DALE (*blurting out*): I'm general manager down at J.C. Penny's.

A look from SUE ELLEN.

MONTE (*Jack Webb reading*): Me, I'm a cop.

CHERIE (*sings "Dragnet" theme*): Dum-de-dum-dum. (*They laugh.*)

DALE: No kiddin'.

MONTE: Gonna make sergeant next month.

CHERIE: If you don't fuck up! Oops, pardon my French.

DALE (*after a moment of silence that seems like a year*): Is that . . . er . . . you get hurt in the line of duty?

MONTE (*raising his broken arm and hand*): This? Nah, I got this on my night job. Caught it in a mangle.

SUE ELLEN: Jeepers.

CHERIE: Don't worry, honey, he's as good with one hand as most guys are with two.

SUE ELLEN: I'm sure he is.

All take seats and sip from their drinks. Awkward silence. Then:

MONTE: Well, how's the old wazoo?

DALE (*with nervous laugh*): Fine, thank you. (*Pause.*) Well, O.K. I guess. How long you folks been swingers?

MONTE: Ten years.

CHERIE: You won't believe this, but last week me and Monte celebrated our twenty-fifth weddin' anniversary.

SUE ELLEN: No!

MONTE: Made it all the way to Silver.

CHERIE: Hi-ho Silver! (*She and* MONTE *break up.*)

DALE (*a bit taken aback*): Any kids?

CHERIE: Kids! Why sweetheart, I'm a grandmother! (*She squeezes his knee.*)

DALE (*weakly*): Son of a gun.

CHERIE: Never know it by the firm tits, would you?

MONTE (*taking pictures from his wallet*): Hell, yes. This here is little Donna, I call her "the princess." Isn't she the sweetest thing?

CHERIE: Billy, that's our boy, Donna's daddy, he's with the telephone company.

MONTE: Lineman.

CHERIE (*pointing to another photo*): And here's Tina, she's in the junior college at Wichita. Goin' to be a nurse.

SUE ELLEN: Why, I'd never believe you'd have grandchildren, you look so young.

DALE: Sure must of married young.

CHERIE: It was in high school. I was a junior, Monte was a senior. Well, you know how kids are . . . the first few years we were hotter'n a pistol.

MONTE: Hotter'n a pistol.

CHERIE: We were doin' the dirty deed 'round the clock. But after some time, we just sort of lost our spark. You know how it is, it just got to be a habit. Wham, bam, thank you, ma'am. You know what I mean?

SUE ELLEN: Yup.

DALE *gives her a look.*

CHERIE: Well, we tried juicin' it up. (*With a sentimental laugh.*) We had all sorts of tricks. I'd go to some cocktail lounge and pretend I was a hoo-er. And Monte here would come in actin' out he was a . . .

In spite of herself, SUE ELLEN *gasps out loud.*

You done it too, ain'tcha? Well, don't be embarrassed, honey. If the truth were known, half the action in cocktail lounges is husbands pickin' up their *own* wives. Well then, one fine day I found out that Monte was rootin' around in somebody else's trough. There I'd been home fixin' dinner and he'd be out fuckin' and suckin' to beat the band.

MONTE *chuckles with pride.*

You can laugh now, darlin', but those were dark days. There I was faced with my marriage goin' down the drain. So I up and told him what I knew and he had the face to admit it. I'll always give you credit for that, darlin'. You know how men are, honey. They just gotta get their rocks off in different places. So I says to him, "What about me, I got rocks to get off, too!" Next thing you know, he brought home a magazine with a story on swappin'. (*To* SUE ELLEN.) That's what we used to call swingin' in those days, honey. Swappin'. (*To both of them again.*) So we started correspondin' with other couples and got to know nearly every swinger from thirty miles around, some of the finest people you'd ever want to meet. I don't mean folks where you just come in and lay your pecker on the table, I mean *good* people. (*With a warm smile.*) And I just know that includes Y—O—U.

SUE ELLEN: Aren't you the sweetest thing.

MONTE: Well, let's get the ball rollin'. Five more minutes of this and I'll have to start beatin' the bishop!

CHERIE *laughs appreciatively.* MONTE *picks up airline bag, unzips it, pulls out a deck of cards.*

SUE ELLEN: Strip poker?

CHERIE: These ain't regular playin' cards, honey. It's what's known as an "action deck."

MONTE: We picked 'em up from a Mex last summer vacation. (*In a Mexican accent:*) Fifty-two cards. Fifty-two pictures.

CHERIE: Fifty-two positions!

DALE *starts going through the deck, his eyes widening in lust; he is starting to squirm. Then, without looking up, he hands* SUE ELLEN *some.*

SUE ELLEN'S *eyes pop; she is as fascinated as her husband as she begins to look at the pictures;* MONTE *and* CHERIE *exchange assured glances.*

SUE ELLEN (*stopping at one card which absolutely fascinates her; to* CHERIE): My Lord! Doesn't that hurt?

CHERIE: Sure, a little.

DALE (*man of the world*): You know—

CHERIE: I think it's about time we had some music. Put on somethin' real dreamy, Dale.

DALE (*goes to stereo cabinet, records are already*

stacked): I'm way ahead of you.

Music begins and the two couples begin to dance, very close, hardly moving. MONTE *begins to turn it on, a very heavy make. He strokes* SUE ELLEN, *nuzzles her neck, really works her over. She is not objecting; in fact, she is putty in his hands—a whole part of her, long hidden, coming to life. He puts his good hand on her ass now.*

SUE ELLEN (*in a shaky voice*): Oooooo . . .

MONTE: You like that, huh? Nothin' wrong with that, sweet thing.

And with that he unzips the back of her hostess pyjamas, slides his hand in and onto her ass under the cloth; she is melting. Meanwhile, DALE *has been torn between watching this and getting very horny from the attentions of* CHERIE, *who is grinding her tits against him and rubbing all over. Slowly she turns his head away from watching* SUE ELLEN.

CHERIE: Don't worry about them, hon. They're doin' just fine.

She grinds against him. He reacts.

CHERIE (*feeling his hard-on*): IF YOU GOT IT, FLAUNT IT!!

DALE *gives himself up to the sexiness of the dance;* CHERIE *begins playing with his shirt buttons while he kisses her ear. She opens the top two buttons of his shirt, slides her hand in, begins massaging his bare chest. Suddenly* DALE *looks very tense; it is all too much for him; he is way ahead of his fantasy and we begin to realize how close he is to coming already.*

DALE: No, no . . . stop, stop . . . don't, don't don't . . . I'm goin' to . . . no . . . ohno, ohno, ohno . . . OHH!

And DALE *has an orgasm, as* CHERIE *looks on amazed. The two others stop at the noise and see immediately what has happened.*

SUE ELLEN (*furious*): Oh no! You didn't!

MONTE (*amused*): Jumped the gun, didn't you, buddy?

DALE (*after recovering; he is, of course, mortified*): Oh
God, I'm sorry . . . I, I just couldn't help . . . I'm
sorry, I'm real, real sorry.

SUE ELLEN (*disgusted with him*): For Pete's sake.

DALE (*who has to get out fast (a) because he wants to
and (b) because he has to*): Look now, I'll, I'll be
O.K. in a little while . . . just gimme a few minutes . . .

SUE ELLEN (*she knows better*): *Sure* you will, tiger.

DALE (*dying of shame*): Well, I didn't mean to. I'll be
right back, O.K.? (*And he exits swiftly into bedroom
in a very awkward manner, walking like a man who
has . . . well, like a man who has come in his pants.*)

MONTE: He always that quick on the trigger?

SUE ELLEN (*clenched teeth*): It's been known to happen.

MONTE (*expansively*): Well, don't let it worry you.
Hell, wait'll you meet Tom Harris—he comes when
you look at him.

CHERIE: But that don't matter. He'll do French Culture
for you till the cows come home.

SUE ELLEN: French Culture?

And with that MONTE *pulls her down on the couch
which faces away from the audience, so that all we
can hear are the murmurs and appreciative moans
that begin now to come from* SUE ELLEN. CHERIE,
*abandoned, walks over to the couch, whose occu-
pants we cannot see, and abstractedly dipping a Frito
in onion-cheese dip, begins to eat slowly as she
watches. The moans and sighs grow hotter. Finally:*

CHERIE (*she can't take it anymore*): I don't give a
G.D! I ain't gonna miss out on this action! (*And she
peels off her blouse and jumps on the couch with the
other two.*)

*Now all we can hear are noises from the couch and
all we can see are arms and legs which appear now
and then. After a bit of this, enter* DALE *from bedroom. He has put on a fresh pair of slacks. For a
moment he doesn't realize what is going on.*

43

DALE: Everything O.K.?

Now he sees them on the couch. Slowly, amazed, he walks over and looks. SUE ELLEN *lets out a soulful cry.*

MONTE (*speaking thickly*): Hey, buddy, hand me that bag, will you?

MONTE *gestures impatiently.* DALE *hands him the airline bag;* MONTE *disappears from sight. We hear the zipper open.* MONTE *appears again with a plug in his hand. To* DALE:

MONTE: Plug this in, will you?

DALE: What are you goin' to do with *that!*

SUE ELLEN (*her voice from the couch*): JUST PLUG IT IN, YOU DODO!

And so DALE *walks to the wall with the plug and*

*extension cord, bends down, and plugs it in. He looks
miserable. The minute the plug is in, a loud buzzing
sound emanates from behind the couch, followed in-
stantly by the wild ecstatic shrieks of both* SUE ELLEN
and CHERIE. DALE *can barely bring himself to look.
He glances there for a moment, looks as if he's ready
to weep. Then, shoulders slumped, he stands in the
living room, completely out of what is taking place
behind him, staring around, the fifth wheel, wishing
he could go but knowing that he'd better not. He
walks over to sofa in front of the coffee table, sits
down heavily. Sighs and moans and flailing limbs
continue. Slowly, he picks up the deck of pornographic playing cards and stares at them dully. He
begins to deal himself a game of solitaire.*

CURTAIN

45

Jack and Jill

The people of the play:
JACK: *who is about 27 more or less.*
JILL: *who is a few years younger than that, either way.*

Where they are: An isolated area. There is a pile of golden alphabet blocks in the center of it.

As the scene is changing, the song:

> Jack and Jill are playing games
> And they are young and bright
> And impossibly beautiful.
> Their whole world is warm and loving
> So Jack and Jill will play their games forever.
> Jack and Jill will play their games forever.

Note: JACK *is dressed in a yellow suit, a yellow shirt, a black mod necktie, and white shoes.* JILL *is all dressed up in yellow too, except for a white belt, white shoes, and tiny white gloves.* JACK *and* JILL *enter.* JILL *is giggling merrily, half-running ahead of* JACK; *he looks happily surprised.*

JILL: This is it, Jack! This is it! Isn't it just simply beautiful?

JACK: It really is, Jill, it really is beautiful.

JILL: Is it better than what I described to you?

JACK: A whole lots better.

JILL: A whole lots better than that cocktail party.

JACK: You can't even compare it to that dumb cocktail party.

47

JILL: And a whole lots better than that dinner party.

JACK: That was the stupidest dinner party I've ever been to.

JILL: And certainly a whole lots better than that orgy party.

JACK: Do you know, that was the corniest dinner and orgy party I've ever been to.

JILL *begins to walk around the outside of the alphabet block area.*

JILL: I'm beginning to hate cocktail parties, dinner parties, and orgy parties.

JACK *begins to follow a few feet behind her.*

JACK: I am too, Jill. Especially the orgy parties. The dumb stupid orgy parties.

JILL: Dumb and stupid.

JACK: And that's why we're both here; because we're both not dumb, and we're both not stupid.

JILL: We're very bright, and we're very impossibly beautiful.

JACK: It's a wonderful place. But what can we do in it?

JILL: Well, we could have a cocktail party. Or a dinner party. Or an orgy party. It certainly wouldn't be like any of the ones we've been to. We could have them alone.

JACK *immediately kisses* JILL *on the lips.*

JILL: Oh, God, Jack!

JACK: What's the matter, Jill?

JILL: Well, maybe we shouldn't have done that.

JACK: Why?

JILL: Well, we just met this afternoon. Maybe we should get to know one another a little bit more first.

JACK *tries to kiss her again, but she pushes him away and runs up the alphabet blocks to her swing.*

JACK: I'm sorry, Jill.

JILL (*from the swing*): It's too late now.

JACK: Will you stop that, Jill?

JILL: Why should I, Jack?

JACK: I told you I was sorry.

JILL: It's not enough.

JACK: Then what am I supposed to do?

JILL: I don't know.

JACK: Give me an idea.

JILL: Don't you have an imagination?

JACK: It's all I got, Jill. My imagination. Oh, and I forgot! I got one other thing.

JILL: What is it, Jack?

JACK: I got my imagination and I got my cock. And that's all I got, Jill.

JILL stops swinging. She blocks her ears with her hands.

But I suppose that's enough for a man to have: an imagination and a cock.

JILL: Your mouth should be washed out with soap!

JACK: What's the matter with you, Jill?! What are you scared of?

JILL: I'm scared of *you.*

JACK: Me? Why are you scared of me?

JILL: Well, it's because . . . because . . . you're a boy!

JACK: Because I'm a boy? Of course I'm a boy. And you're a girl. I'm not scared of you because you're a girl, am I? And so why should you be scared of me?

JILL: Because you're a boy, a man, and you just want me for kissing and other things . . .

JACK: Aw, c'mon!

JILL: After you get through playing with me, you'll get tired of me and look for another girl to play with.

JACK: You got the wrong idea about everything, Jill. There's nothing to be scared of.

JACK stands in front of JILL and then he kisses her. It is long and loving and JILL gives in to the kiss. The music for JACK and JILL begins to play again.

JILL: Jack, Jack, Jack. Please say that you love me. Please tell me that you are in love with me. Please let me know that you'll stay in love with me for as long as forever is.

JACK: You're not scared anymore, are you, Jill? You're really beautiful, Jill.

49

JILL: I think you're adorable, Jack.

JACK: What shall we do?

JILL: I don't know.

JACK: What would you like to do?

JILL: Anything you want to do, Jack. After all, you're the boy. It's all up to you. I'm just the girl.

JACK: Do you want to play measuring?

JILL: Measuring?

JACK: It's a game that I made up all by myself. Only a girl and a boy can play it.

JILL: Well, then: we can play it, can't we?

JACK: Sure.

JILL: Will it be fun for me?

JACK: Yes. Lots of fun for both of us.

JILL: What's it about?

JACK: It's about . . . well . . . it's about . . . love, I guess . . .

JILL: Love? Oh, that's nice already.

JACK: Now here's what we do. We get a ruler, first, see? You must have a ruler someplace around here, don't you?

JILL: In my pencil box! (JILL *runs to the blocks and finds her pencil box. She dumps everything out of it.*) Here it is, Jack! It's a twelve-inch ruler. That's enough, isn't it?

JACK: Well, we'll see, Jill. (*Takes ruler in his hands.*)

JILL: I can hardly wait!

JACK: Don't get so excited. Save being excited for when we're really playing the last part of the game.

JILL: Well, just hurry up and tell me how to play it, that's all.

JACK: We take turns, see? It doesn't matter whose turn it is first. But since you're the girl, well, I think it should be your turn first.

JILL: That's nice of you, Jack.

JACK: What you do is this: you take the ruler and you measure my thing first to see how long it is and then . . .

JILL: Your thing?

JACK: My thing. There's nothing wrong with that.

JILL: Oh, Jack.

JACK: C'mon, Jill.

JILL: But don't you already know how long it is? I mean you must have played this game with other girls before me. So you must know how long it is.

JACK: I swear to God that I never played this game with any other girl in my whole life.

JILL: Oh, Jack, what am I going to do with you? You're really impossible.

JACK: And then, after you measure my thing, I take the ruler and I slowly, carefully, gently, slip it into your thing in order to see how deep it is.

JILL: Oh, God, Jack.

JACK: And if your thing is deeper than my thing is long, then you have the right to decide whether you want my thing to slide inside you or not, and if my thing is longer then *I* decide.

JILL: Oh, God, Jack.

JACK: And that's it, Jill. I told you it was easy.

JILL: I'm scared, Jack.

JACK: Please, don't be, O.K., Jill? Jill . . . ? O.K. . . . ?

JILL: But . . . well . . . Jack . . . ?

JACK: Yes?

JILL: Doesn't your thing . . . doesn't it . . . doesn't your thing have to be . . . up in the air . . . if you really want it measured the right way? Oh, Jack, I'm so ashamed!

JACK: It is up in the air! It's been standing up in the air ever since I first met you this afternoon.

JILL: Oh, God, Jack.

JACK: C'mon, Jill.

The JACK *and* JILL *music begins to play.* JACK *takes* JILL *reluctantly behind the alphabet blocks. The lights get very bright and golden now.*

JILL: Oh, God, Jack!

JACK: You see?

JILL: Oh, good God, Jack!

JACK: The ruler! C'mon, use the ruler!

JILL: Oh, Jack . . .

JACK: That's it, Jill. That's it!

51

JILL: I feel funny, Jack.

JACK: How much is it, Jill? How much?!

JILL: Oh, God . . . Jack . . . ?

JACK: How many inches, Jill?

JILL: It's . . . it's . . .

JACK: C'mon, Jill.

JILL: Six! It's a little over six inches. Oh, Jack! God!

JACK: That's not bad. It could be a lot better. But it's not that bad, is it, Jill? Now it's my turn to measure your thing, Jill.

JILL: Oh, Jack, maybe you better not!

JACK: I promise you: it won't hurt.

JILL: Please . . . be careful, Jack!

JACK: Nothing to worry about . . . nothing, Jill, nothing.

JILL: Ohhhhhhhhhh . . .

JACK: Be still, Jill . . .

JILL: I can't.

JACK: You've got to be, Jill.

JILL: Ohhhhhhhhhh . . . Jack . . . Ohhhhhhhhh . . .

JACK: There . . . you see . . . Jill?

JILL: Ohhhhhh . . . ahhhhhh . . . Ohhhhhh, Jack, I think it's . . . as far as it can go!

JACK: I think you're right, Jill.

JILL: How much, Jack? How much?!

JACK: Well . . .

JILL: Did I win?

JACK: Well . . .

JILL: I did, didn't I? Didn't I?

JACK: It's exactly eight inches deep.

JILL: I won! I won, Jack! I won!

JACK: All right, all right.

> JILL *runs from behind the alphabet blocks. Only* JILL's *music is playing now. She begins to dance by herself.*

JILL: You were so right, Jack.

JACK: So right about what?

JILL: You said it would be lots of fun. And it was, Jack. It was lots of fun!

> JACK *comes out from behind the alphabet blocks.*

JACK: Have you decided yet, Jill?

JILL: Decided?

JACK: Now you've got the choice, remember?! Do I put my thing inside of your thing or not?!

JILL: You're terrible . . .

JACK: Yes or no, Jill?

JILL: I'm in love with you, Jack.

JACK: All right, all right! I'm in love with you too. Now c'mon! What are we going to do?

JILL: I met you only this afternoon, Jack, and I'm positively in love with you, in love with you, in love with you . . . (JILL *lies down half-gracefully on the blocks.*)

JACK: I'm in love with you, too, baby!

JACK *flings himself upon* JILL. *She screams quietly as she goes over on her back.* JACK *kisses her everywhere. She fights back, but it is done almost hopelessly.* JACK *goes on kissing her everywhere. The kisses become more violent.*

JILL: You're hurting me, Jack!

JACK: It's not going to hurt, Jill!

JACK *is wild upon* JILL *now. He tries to get her clothes off. He tries to do it all at the same time, in the same frantic moment.*

JILL: You're killing me, Jack.

JACK *tears off her panties and is completely covering her with his body now, kissing and panting and wild with movement.*

JILL: Oh no! Oh no! Please Jack . . . I'm in love with you, Jack!

JACK: ME TOO, BABY! ME TOO! BABY!

JILL: Oh, good God, good God . . . good God, help me!

JACK: Did you see them all, baby?! Did you see them all at the cocktail party?! Big tits, small tits, almost showing, almost falling out right into my wide-open mouth. I kissed one on the neck from the back while I stuck my hand up her short red shining dress! I'm

in love with you too, BABY! And at the dinner party it was even better, sucking on teaspoons, tablespoons, and sliding their lips on hard sharp forks. And dropping strawberries on my crotch and red wine on my necktie and spilling brandy on my cock! Oh, good God, BABY! And the orgy party?! It wasn't that dumb and it wasn't that stupid! Two girls, really beautiful-looking young girls like fat and healthy fashion models, they took me into the bathroom and . . .

JILL: No, Jack! No, Jack! You're going to kill me!

JACK *lifts* JILL'S *arms up and down, dropping them. He lifts her legs up and down, dropping them. He rubs her stomach. Each new thing becomes more frantic with* JACK. *He kisses her as roughly as possible, everywhere.*

JILL: Jack! Jack! Jack! You don't know what you're doing to me! Jack! . . .! OH. GOOD GOD, NO! (JILL *is suddenly motionless. She lies absolutely still on the alphabet blocks. She is dead.*)

JACK: Hey baby! It wasn't that dumb and stupid! That last party wasn't that dumb and stupid!

The music has stopped completely now.

Hey, baby! What's your name anyway? You never told me your name. My name is Joe. What's your name? So you aren't talking, huh? Well, my name is Richard. Jesus Christ, are you stubborn. My name is Larry. HEY, BABY! *WHAT THE HELL IS YOUR NAME?* I won't hurt you. I'm the gentlest guy you'll ever meet in your whole life. I wouldn't hurt a fly. In fact, I always protect flies and moths, and butterflies, too.

JACK *begins to stroke* JILL'S *body. He is extra-kind, extra-gentle, extra-tender, extra-smooth, extra-careful. He props her body up in a sitting position, very demure, carefully arranging her hands and legs.*

I'll bet I know what your name is. Your name is Jill. I'll bet that's what it is, isn't it: Jill. You look like a

Jill to me. It's a very pretty name for a girl: Jill. I'll bet that's what it is: Jill.

He puts her mouth into a smile, opens her eyes.

How are you, Jill? My name is Jim.

JACK *goes to leave, notices* JILL's *panties, picks them up, twirls them in the air, and turns, leaving the area.*

Song.

END

Delicious Indignities or The Deflowering of Helen Axminster

At rise an elegantly appointed study in Knightsbridge, 1896. A long wall of velvet curtains shuts out the view. A fireplace, with a stuffed tiger's head hanging above it, a roaring fire in the hearth. A wall of leather-bound volumes, an overstuffed French armchair, all attest to the upper-class affluence of ALFRED DUFF-PORTER, *a 30-year-old bachelor.* ALFRED, *a very bland and proper-looking Englishman, sports a very bland and proper-looking blond mustache. He is ushering into the room his guest,* HELEN AXMINSTER, *hanging up her rain cape, dousing her umbrella in a large oriental porcelain pot.* HELEN *is a strikingly pretty girl, with round-eyed innocence in her face, an opulent figure, and a musical voice. The voice, given to arias, runs on with machine-gun speed, but amazing clarity. She is in vigorous good health, dressed in a simple blouse and skirt; a brooch —a large ruby—is set at her neck. She goes immediately to the fire and warms her hands, looking around the room.*

HELEN: What a wonderful room it really is, Alfred. Those curtains, the carpet, and that poofy looking armchair. You bachelors do study your comforts.

ALFRED: Won't you sit down, Helen? Make yourself comfortable?

HELEN: Certainly not, Alfred. It is one thing to make myself dry and cozy by your fire. Quite another to make myself—(*pausing and enunciating disdainfully*) comfortable!

ALFRED: But surely you'll sit down for tea?

HELEN: I am quite capable of holding a cup standing up, Alfred.

ALFRED: Helen, we've known each other since childhood—

HELEN: We are no longer children, Alfred. Indeed, I had grave doubts about coming here today.

ALFRED: You couldn't!

HELEN: An unmarried woman does not take tea in the rooms of bachelor friends, Alfred. I dare say, if the rain hadn't come down with such inexorable force, and your flat so close by, I would never have honored your invitation.

ALFRED: Then I must thank the rain for helping overcome your scruples.

HELEN: Alfred, my scruples were never overcome. They were merely dampened and chilled.

ALFRED (*pouring tea*): Sorry Helen. No offense intended. Milk and sugar?

HELEN: Oh, no thank you, Alfred. It's far healthier to warm from the outside in. Mummy made me vow never to take tea when I am still chilled. Mmmmmm.

ALFRED: But you'll have a bread and butter sandwich?

HELEN: Salt or sweet?

ALFRED: What?

HELEN: The butter, Alfred.

ALFRED: Salt.

HELEN: Pity. Mummy made me vow I would never take a salt butter sandwich. They can't be trusted, Alfred. One can't taste the spoilage. I'll take a Huntley-Palmer digestive biscuit, if you bring it to me in an unopened tin.

ALFRED: Sorry, Helen. I don't have any.

HELEN: Pity. Mummy made me vow . . .

ALFRED: Dear Helen, you've taken more vows than a convent of nuns.

HELEN (*sadly*): All save one, Alfred.

ALFRED: No fault of mine—or half the men in London. You've tormented and jilted us all.

HELEN: One has one's standards, Alfred. And no man has yet convinced me to abandon mine. (*She crosses to closed draperies, peeps out.*) My, how the rain comes pelting down. Yet you can't hear it at all here. It is snug—

ALFRED: I call this room my snuggery.

HELEN (*disapproving*): Do you, Alfred? I think it's rather vulgar to give pet names to places. (*She looks about, now critical, indicating the ropes near the curtains.*) Surely you can find prettier curtain pulls, Alfred? These *are* strange.

ALFRED: I'm sorry they offend you, Helen.

HELEN (*patting his hands indulgently*): Oh, Alfred. You mustn't take everything I say to heart. Show me how to work them so we can look out at the rain, will you?

ALFRED: You really wish to know?

HELEN: Of course, Alfred. It would be so pleasant to watch the rain. Do show me.

ALFRED: It might be difficult, Helen.

HELEN: Nonsense. I used to be captain of the gym at St. Margaret's.

ALFRED: As you wish, Helen.

He places her wrists inside loops. She pulls, and, instead of drapes opening, a spring is snapped and she is whirled around, her wrists pulled out to the side, pinning her back, spread-eagled, against the draperies. She screams. He laughs fiendishly.

HELEN (*astonished*): Alfred, have you gone mad?

ALFRED: No, Helen, I am quite sane.

HELEN: Alfred, I am leaving now!

ALFRED: Helen, you don't imagine that I shall permit you to leave this room until you have satisfied my purpose.

HELEN: What purpose?

ALFRED: Your violation. The surrender of your maidenhead. The conquest of your unassailed virginity.

HELEN: Mr. Duff-Porter. Until you have suitably apologized for this intolerable insult, you may consider our friendship suspended.

ALFRED: My dear Miss Axminster. I fear, until I shall have accomplished my ends, both our friendship *and* your arms are suspended.

HELEN: Alfred—(*Commanding.*) You will recover yourself and call a cab for me.

ALFRED: Helen, rage all you wish. It will do you no good. Don't imagine this is a sudden inspiration. I have spent months preparing for your visit. I took these rooms solely because they would lend themselves so admirably to this end. Your cries and screams cannot be heard outside.

HELEN: But your manservant—

ALFRED: Dismissed until morning.

HELEN: Oh, God—

ALFRED: You must decide now, Helen. What will you do? Submit quietly to me? Or do you prefer to be forced?

HELEN: I will never submit!

ALFRED *approaches her, kisses her mouth passionately, begins to unbutton her blouse. He removes it—folds it neatly as she twists on the ropes. He next removes her skirt—but is forced to rip it off as she struggles with her legs. Finally she is stripped down to her underclothes. He begins to run his hands over her body, down to her thighs, then he strips her naked, except for her knickers.* HELEN, *in a last effort to free herself from his attentions, raises her knees and kicks him fiercely, hurling him backwards into the comfortable chair. As he falls into the chair, its arms snap across his chest, locking him inside the chair, stunned.*

ALFRED (*desperately*): You bloody bitch! Look what you've done.

HELEN: Release me, immediately.

ALFRED: I can't release you. I can't even release myself.

HELEN: Nonsense.

ALFRED: This chair was specially made for me in France . . .

HELEN: Alfred, I know all I wish to know about your furniture.

ALFRED: It's a duplicate of the Marquis de Sade's chair of treachery. As soon as one rests one's weight in it, it locks you in.

HELEN: And you meant it for me?

ALFRED: Only if you wouldn't try the curtain pulls.

HELEN: You had no right to undertake a project of such dimensions—unless you were prepared for all the eventualities. (*Remembering.*) Oh God—what shall I ever tell Mummy?

ALFRED: I'm sorry, Helen.

HELEN: Surely, you've done better by your other victims.

ALFRED: Please, Helen, there were no other victims.

HELEN (*outraged*): You mean I was to be your first? That shows you had no respect for my position. A gentleman would have practiced on his maid, you bungling fool!

ALFRED: Helen, that isn't kind.

HELEN: What do you know of kindness, Alfred?

ALFRED: Believe me, Helen, no man has ever cared for you as much as I. To take such risks—

HELEN: Rot! Do you think your feeble effort was the first attempt upon the fortress of my virtue.

ALFRED (*irate*): Who would dare to—

HELEN: Ha? Many have dared, Alfred—but all have failed. I have never submitted to any man—

ALFRED: Brave girl, Helen—

HELEN: Oh God—if you were only more like Sir Harry Yelverton—

ALFRED: What has Sir Harry to do with our predicament?

HELEN: Sir Harry had the honor of being the first man to try my innocence and fail.

ALFRED: That devil! No wonder they call him the Fox of Fleet Street.

Lights dim on room, spot on HELEN: *the light acts as the specter of Sir Harry. It plays upon those parts of her body under attack.*

I was scarcely fourteen when Sir Harry invited Mummy and me down to Surrey for the weekend. We were going to ride—but Mummy would have her headache and I went off alone, with Sir Harry. A sudden storm broke, lightning flashed, my stallion bolted for the stable. I could scarcely control the beast. Sir Harry galloped after me and helped me to dismount. Suddenly, I saw him signal to his groom, who closed the stable door and bolted it from the outside. "Sir Harry," I cried, "what is the meaning of this?" "Be calm, my child," he replied. "You are only going to be stripped naked." "But why?" I asked. "In order to learn how a girl controls a stallion!" he replied. Imagine my anguish as garment after garment was removed by Sir Harry. At last, I was left naked, save for my riding boots. He, too, decided to tie my arms. "Don't! Don't!" I cried. But his reply was to stroke most lovingly my delicious twin globes. Then he threw me down upon the hay, reluctantly quitting my maiden breasts with a passionate kiss upon the terrified nipples. My eyes dilated with horror as he vigorously attacked my thighs, his hand descending into the moist mysteries of my virgin recesses.

ALFRED: The filthy child molester! Poor Helen—fingered and not yet fifteen.

HELEN: His bold fingers were but the rude couriers of a blind tyrant. The violation proceeded—mindless of my pleading—as stiff and rampant, that ruler rioted within my outraged orifice. Now, a strange and alien sensation occurred within me—

ALFRED (shocked): Not pleasure, Helen?

HELEN: How dare you suggest that, Alfred? I was merely overcome. Naturally, I fainted.

ALFRED: Thank God!

HELEN: Now I arrive at that part which may be instructive to you. When I regained consciousness, I found myself scrubbed clean, neatly dressed, not a strand of straw on my person to testify to the assault. Why, even my boots were polished to the highest gloss. Graciously, Sir Harry escorted me to Mummy in the manor house. He recommended that I be sent upstairs to nap, since the storm had quite unsettled my nerves.

ALFRED (angrily): Of course you told your mother of the outrage?

HELEN: I did not!

ALFRED: But he raped you!

HELEN: What had that to do with me, Alfred? I had not voluntarily submitted. I had struggled in a fashion befitting my age and education. Should I abandon the honored state of virgin for the indecent condition of victim? Naturally, I kept my own counsel. And a wise move it was. The following spring, Sir Harry arranged for Daddy to be appointed to a high government post in India. What a blessing that was, Alfred—in spite of the Rajah.

ALFRED: The Rajah?

HELEN: It was beastly hot in Poonah, so Mummy and Daddy sent me to spend a few weeks with the Rajah, at his summer palace in the hills. A charming but

uneventful stay. The Rani—a dear brown creature—
the Raj—a splendid host.

ALFRED: Helen, what happened?

HELEN: It was the day of my leavetaking. I kissed the
Rani goodbye on her adorable red caste mark—then
I ventured to the summer garden to say farewell to
my host. It was there that he announced his intention of showing me a view of India denied to most
foreign women. At which point, he undid his white
silk mohair trousers, and revealed his rising regality.
I attempted to flee the garden. My way was blocked
by six huge servants, who dragged me, fighting
and shrieking, back to the Rajah. My struggles were
useless. I was a reed caught in a monsoon. And I
was forced to witness the Rajah as he anointed his
lingham.

ALFRED: Good Lord!

HELEN: He advised me that he was applying a mixture
of ground thorn apple, black pepper, and honey—a
recipe which his cruel oriental tradition had pre-
scribed for the violation of virgins. I was now forced
to lie down, upon some very pretty slubbed silk
cushions, while his servants spread my legs apart, in
order, as he said, to widen my yoni!

ALFRED: Your yoni?

HELEN (ignoring him): My legs were placed in what he
called the yawning position—forced to rest upon the
Rajah's broad shoulders. Suddenly, from between
his clenched ivory teeth, he issued the sound "Phut!"
at which point he struck me softly across the breasts
—while penetrating to my depths.

ALFRED: You poor child!

HELEN: Alfred, you cannot imagine the torment I endured beneath the Rajah's raging lust. Only when he
had satisfied his cruel craving, in what he called the
Congress of the Cow, was I permitted to rest.

ALFRED: He took you like an animal!

HELEN (fiercely): A sacred animal, Alfred. Remember
that! When it was over, he summoned an elderly,
turbaned scholar. The man arrived bearing calipers.
With these, a careful measure of my outraged inno-

cence was taken. Another servant was summoned. He returned with a jewel, a large ruby, which, the Rajah informed me, was the exact circumference of my yoni. Very gently, I was placed upon a splendid white elephant to begin my journey back to Poonah —with a company of Ghurka soldiers as escorts.

ALFRED: Poor Helen—what you have endured.

HELEN: Without complaint, Alfred. It does no good to fret about the unavoidable, does it? Why, in my travels I have been attacked and outraged over thirty-seven times. (*Ticking them off.*) A Methodist minister in Minehead. A decadent dealer in snuff boxes in Brighton . . . two terrible tinkers in Tunbridge Wells . . . to name but a few. But I have had the will to suffer them all—and remain chaste! Never once have I been compromised by an attacker. Never once has a whisper been raised about the virtue of Helen Axminster. Never once (*grieving*) until now!

ALFRED: Helen, I swear, I'll never breathe a word—

HELEN: What good will that do, Alfred. I will have spent the night in your flat—

ALFRED: Without incident, Helen.

HELEN: What difference will that make, Alfred? When we are freed tomorrow, I will no longer be a virgin. You have ruined me, Alfred.

ALFRED: But I never—

HELEN: I will be removed from my position at the head of Mayfair society and placed directly in its crotch.

ALFRED: Helen—you merely imagine—

HELEN: I know the world, Alfred. And it speaks with a foul mouth about girls who permit themselves to be compromised. She becomes the source of hideous alliteration—all cock and cunt—all prick and pussy—all ruthless rutting.

ALFRED (*shocked*): Helen—don't!

HELEN: I have been ambushed by an amateur in an imitation antique armchair. (*She weeps.*)

ALFRED: Helen—is there no remedy?

HELEN: None! (*Considering.*) Unless—no—but still—perhaps—

ALFRED: Yes, Helen?

HELEN (*shaping plan*): Tomorrow, when your man comes to release us—I will not return home to Mummy.

ALFRED: Helen—what are you saying?!

HELEN: We will go to Scotland to be married!

ALFRED: Married? You don't think I would marry you after—

HELEN: Scotland, Alfred—or Scotland Yard! Fortunately, you live close to Harrod's, Alfred, so I can purchase my trousseau in the morning and we can elope by noon. Perhaps it's for the best. After all, one can't remain a virgin forever—one risks becoming a spinster. (*To herself.*) Yes, it's time, Helen Axminster. Time to lower the drawbridge and let the enemy enter. Gone, all gone. Gone forever are those delicious indignities. (*Through her tears.*) I'm sure we shall be very happy, Alfred.

CURTAIN

Was It Good For You Too?

PERLMUTTER (*addresses audience*): So this ad said they were looking for healthy young guys, and I didn't have too much work to do. So I figured what the hell, you know? (*He walks stage right where there is a desk with chair.*)

INTERVIEWER (*female*): Good afternoon.

PERLMUTTER: Good afternoon. (*Pause.*) I'm here about the . . . the experiment.

INTERVIEWER: Ah.

PERLMUTTER: The one you mentioned in the ad?

INTERVIEWER: You're a student here?

PERLMUTTER: Yes, Pre-med.

INTERVIEWER: Tell me, why are you volunteering to participate in a sex experiment?

PERLMUTTER: Well, outside of the obvious *professional* interest I have in such activity . . .

INTERVIEWER: Yes, outside of that.

PERLMUTTER: Well, quite frankly, I consider myself somewhat of a . . . actually, *quite* a good . . . uh, well, at least a fairly adequate lover, and . . .

INTERVIEWER: And . . .

PERLMUTTER: And also, I thought it might be a good way of meeting girls.

INTERVIEWER: You understand, of course, that you will never be permitted to learn the identity of the young lady or ladies whom you will, ah, meet during the course of the experiment?

71

PERLMUTTER: That's O.K.

INTERVIEWER: And you understand that the payment of twenty-five dollars is your sole compensation and the full extent of any and all liability incurred as a result of this experiment?

PERLMUTTER: I do.

INTERVIEWER: Very well, take these forms with you, and fill them out in the next room.

Blackout. Lights up on desk with chair, stage left. A girl in a lab coat sits behind it. She is riffling through some forms.

DR. BRONSON: Perlmutter?

PERLMUTTER: Right.

DR. BRONSON: Says here you're volunteering for a straight Hetero-Norm-Coital set-up. That right?

PERLMUTTER: Uh, right.

DR. BRONSON: No interest in any . . . in anything more exotic?

PERLMUTTER: What do you mean?

DR. BRONSON: As I'm sure you realize, not everybody in the world gets his kicks from just genital contact, nor from contact with a partner of a sex opposite to his own, nor from just one partner at a time, nor even from exclusively *human* partners.

PERLMUTTER: Well, naturally.

DR. BRONSON: So what I am asking is whether you truly wish to restrict yourself to a straight coital contact with just one human partner at a time of the opposite sex?

PERLMUTTER: Oh. Well, yes. I believe so.

DR. BRONSON: All right.

PERLMUTTER: At least for the first one.

DR. BRONSON: You realize, of course, that you are going to be observed at all times during the experiment by a team of scientists and a battery of delicate and comprehensive measuring equipment.

PERLMUTTER: I realize that.

DR. BRONSON: Do you think you will be distracted by being observed while in the act of coitus? That is, do you think it will, ah, impair your function?

PERLMUTTER: I doubt it. I've been observed before.

DR. BRONSON: Oh?

PERLMUTTER: I mean, I did live in a fraternity for almost four years.

DR. BRONSON: Very well, take these forms and fill them out.

PERLMUTTER: Thank you.

DR. BRONSON: To save time, you might strip down to your shorts while you're filling out the forms. We're on a tight schedule here.

Blackout. Lights up stage right. A bank of complicated machinery. DR. BRONSON *enters, together with* DR. JASPERS *(male), a male* ATTENDANT, *and a* NURSE.

The tone of the play changes course at this point, almost to the madness of a Marx Bros. film. The male ATTENDANT, *especially, is taken directly from the Harpo Marx characterizations of the Thirties film musicals. The staging is in total keeping with this concept.*

DR. JASPERS: Perlmutter?

PERLMUTTER: Yes.

DR. JASPERS: I'm Dr. Jaspers.

PERLMUTTER *extends his hand to shake* DR. JASPERS'.

DR. JASPERS *(slaps* PERLMUTTER'S *hand aside, grabs the papers from him)*: Just give me the forms. Nurse, send in our other participant.

NURSE *wheels* GIRL *in on high platform table. The* GIRL *is wearing lace bikini panties and brassiere.* PERLMUTTER *gives her a tentative wave "Hello."*

DR. JASPERS *(to* PERLMUTTER*)*: Very well now, will you step over to the table, please? And Dr. Bronson, will you please attach the electrodes?

PERLMUTTER *approaches the table shyly.* DR. BRONSON *approaches the table with several coils of wire, a roll of tape, and a small bottle of clear liquid.*

DR. BRONSON: Don't worry about me, kids, just get started.

PERLMUTTER: What are these things?

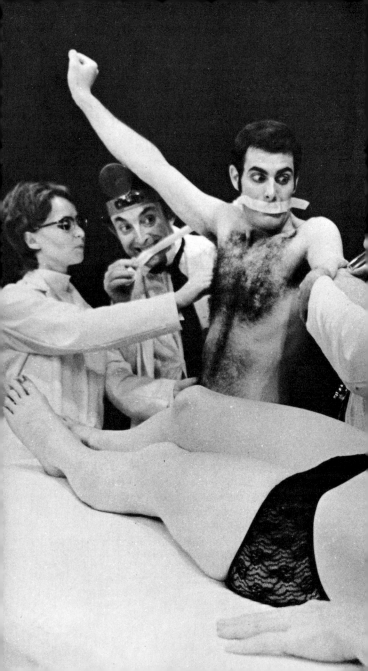

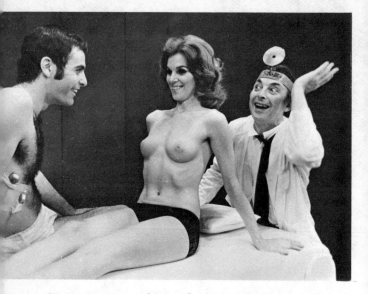

Male ATTENDANT *begins fitting an electrode to the left corner of* PERLMUTTER'S *mouth.*

DR. BRONSON: Don't pay any attention to them. Just get the ball rolling.

PERLMUTTER (*out of the corner of his mouth*): Look, these things are going to get in the way.

ATTENDANT *begins to attach a second electrode to his armpit.*

DR. BRONSON: They shouldn't.

PERLMUTTER: I'm not sure I like these things at all.

DR. BRONSON (*to* GIRL): Then why don't *you* start things off, dear?

The GIRL *reaches out, places her arms around* PERL-MUTTER'S *neck and draws him down on top of her.*

PERLMUTTER: Hello there.

GIRL: Hi. (*She bites his earlobe.*)

DR. BRONSON (*to the* ATTENDANT): Would you please remove the bra? I need a nipple here.

76 ℘ *Was It Good for You Too?*

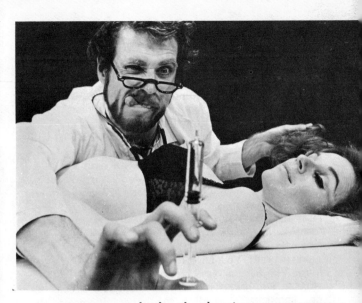

ATTENDANT *unhooks the brassiere.* PERLMUTTER *fondles a breast.*

If it's all the same to you, I'd prefer that you worked on the right one. The left one is mine.

PERLMUTTER: Oh, sorry.

GIRL: Mmmmm.

PERLMUTTER: Feel nice?

NURSE: I get an excitation reading of three-point-two. I call that feeling pretty nice.

DR. BRONSON: Let's push on now. I need the crotch.

ATTENDANT *pulls off her panties.* PERLMUTTER *kneels before her, rather dumbfounded.*

DR. BRONSON: Excuse me. You kids may have all night, but we're on a schedule here.

ATTENDANT *rips off* PERLMUTTER'S *shorts.* PERLMUTTER *and the young woman look politely beyond each other's nakedness as the* ATTENDANT *continues to attach electrodes.*

PERLMUTTER: Do you, uh, come here often?

GIRL: I've been here about sixteen or seventeen times.

PERLMUTTER: Oh. Me too. How did you happen to vol—Hey! (*To* DR. BRONSON:) What the hell are you glueing to me *there*?

DR. BRONSON: Merely an interuterine camera. Don't get so upset.

PERLMUTTER: Upset! How do you expect me to—

DR. BRONSON: Did you or did you not tell me that you have extraordinary powers of concentration?

PERLMUTTER: Well, sure, but there's a limit to—

GIRL (*reassuringly*): It's all right, don't worry about it. We'll do it anyway. I'll help you. (*Then she closes her eyes and he kisses her for the first time.*)

PERLMUTTER: You know, you're really very nice. (*He moves his hands over her body.*)

GIRL: So are you.

PERLMUTTER: You have lovely skin.

GIRL: You have a very . . . wiry chest.

NURSE: You have static on your oral-audio circuits.

DR. BRONSON: According to the secretiometer, she doesn't look very excited to me. Young man, do you think you could pep up your pace a little?

PERLMUTTER *peps up his pace. The* GIRL *begins to moan with pleasure.*

NURSE: Contact.

PERLMUTTER *and the* GIRL *are moving rhythmically together.*

Musical vamp. DR. BRONSON *and* NURSE, *nearly oblivious to the action around them, begin to sing in the fashion of a Thirties film musical.*

DR. BRONSON *and* NURSE:
   I like the look

That comes over a
  girl
Who's just been
  kissed.
I like the look
Which announces
That she cannot re-
  sist.
I like the look
That reveals what
  they both are
  thinking of

NURSE:
I wish people would
  leave

BOTH:
Their hearts on
  their sleeve
Because I like the

look of love.

PERLMUTTER: Do you like it like this?

GIRL: Oh, yes. I never knew it could be like this.

DR. BRONSON:
Some people like painting—

NURSE:
Great art never dies . . .

PERLMUTTER: You really think I'm that good?

BOTH:
But I find I prefer
A him and a her

In a frame made of
Kisses and sighs.

GIRL: Marvelous. One of the two best sexual experiences I've had in my entire life.

PERLMUTTER: Who was the other?

GIRL: What?

PERLMUTTER: You said I was one of the *two* best. Who was the other? I have to know.

GIRL: A guy in Wisconsin. I don't even remember his name. But you're better than him. Technically, I mean.

PERLMUTTER: I am, eh? Am I going to see you again?

GIRL: Yes! Yes!

PERLMUTTER: Often?

GIRL: As often as you want. Oh God God God God God.

PERLMUTTER: And will you

DR. BRONSON *and*
NURSE:
I like the look
Of the moon
As it shines on
. lovers' lane.
I like the look
Of a couple ro-
mancing in the
rain.

I like the look
Of two people
Who know what
they're dreaming
of.

NURSE:
So I stroll through
the park

DR. BRONSON:
When it's just get-
ting dark
Because I like the
look

PERLMUTTER *and*
GIRL:
We like the look

DR. BRONSON, DR.
JASPERS *and* NURSE:
They like the look

stop seeing anybody else
you're now seeing?
GIRL: Yes, yes, my God—yes!

*A band of gypsies enters
from stage left, with their
two dogs. Paying abso-
lutely no attention to the
action on stage (and not
getting any attention from
the other occupants of the
stage, with the exception
of the male* ATTENDANT,
*who seems to be quite
taken with one of the dogs
in the group), they circle
the action, passionately
playing the tambourine,
violin, and concertina—in-
struments which they have
far from mastered. In fact,
they've more than likely
never played them before
in their lives, but the noise
they're emitting is music to
their ears. They exit as
rapidly and as unnoticed as
they entered.*

PERLMUTTER: By the way, I
don't believe I caught your
name.
DR. JASPERS: That's not allowed!

of love!

BLACKOUT

Much Too Soon

A tender idyllic piece which begins with the group, naked, bunched together center. The song begins:

Slowly.

I was walking
In the shadows
And the birds were flying to the moon.
Oh life is over
Much too soon.

Don't watch for the morning,
It's only the sun,
And spring is a feeling
Of never run.

I was looking
For a window
And the lamps were covered in the room.
Oh life is over
Much too soon.

Don't wish for a lover,
It's only a friend,
And time is a feeling
Of never end.

And the world keeps floating
All alone in space.
Don't stare at the mirror
It's only your face.

We wait for the echo,
That answers the tune,
And we are over
Much too soon.

The group sways to the slow rhythms as film comes on upstage. The film focuses on faces of the couples as they touch one another innocently, carefully, and then mirrors the movements they will be making during the dance. First KATIE moves out of the group, alone, cold and sad. Couples begin to form. LEON picks BONI up and moves downstage with her in his arms. NANCY, RAINA, and MARK come together and are joined by BILL. The mood of this exploration of sensuality is slow and tender. ALAN, seeing KATIE alone, walks to her, takes her in his arms, holds her. MARGO moves off,

taking GEORGE *with her, but there is a tension in this relationship which will continue during the piece. They never get together—not now.* MARK *reaches to* GEORGE *as he moves off but* GEORGE *is gone.* BILL *moves down toward* LEON *and* BONI, *touching them, watching them as they explore one another. Then* BILL *goes off with* NANCY *and they stroll together slowly around the stage.* MARK *and* RAINA *start to move off toward the side,* RAINA *reaching out toward* GEORGE *as she does, but* MARGO *moves between* GEORGE *and* RAINA. RAINA *continues on with* MARK *and they lie down, softly touching*

one another. LEON and BONI *move off to the other side,*
caressing one another. ALAN *and* KATIE *move upstage,*
stop, kneel, and kiss. BILL *and* NANCY *have encircled*
the stage; they also stop, kneel, and hold each other
very closely. Now the groupings are symmetrical. Down
left, BONI *and* LEON *are lying down, kissing; down right,*
MARK *and* RAINA *are lying down touching one another;*
up left BILL *and* NANCY *kneel, kissing; up right,* KATIE
and ALAN *also kneel, kissing.* GEORGE *and* MARGO *have*
slowly been circling one another, not meeting, keeping
their distance. They stop up center, keeping away from
one another. Everyone freezes in Rodin statue-like poses
as the song comes to an end: "We wait for the echo that
answers the tune, and we are over much too soon". In
the film, the sun slowly rises.

Blackout

Spotlight on MARGO *and* GEORGE, *now facing each other.
The other couples, in semi-darkness, slowly get up and
back offstage, a little tearfully leaving* GEORGE *and*
MARGO *alone. They slowly, almost painfully, reach to
touch one another's face. When they touch, music comes
in: "Clarence and Mildred", a funky, country blues, and
the dance, ONE ON ONE, begins.*

ꝱ One on One

A funky country blues pas de deux.

1. It was mid-week in mid-May
   In the middle 1960's,
   On a fair to middlin' day
   In middle village USA
   That two people, name of Clarence Cooze
   And Mildred Susan Archer,
   Came to be familiar
   In a most familiar way.

2. Along the skin of sixty-six
   Clarence gunned his Harley,
   Nothin' much o' consequence
   Workin' in his head;
   Man and cycle joined together,
   One black mass o' steel and leather,
   A modern metal monster
   For the citizens to dread.

Oh Clarence, hey watch yourself boy, lookee
Mind your fortune cookie, Clarence.

3. Mildred middle-class workin' hard
   Slingin' hash to truckers,
   Suffers 'em to pinch her ass
   And raise her tips that way;
   Then she takes her increased earnin's
   To her lawful husband Vernon
   (Who is unemployed and drinkin' hard
   At Bertha's hideaway.)

91

4. This night she left the diner,
   Lookin' forward to the late show,
   Tuckered out and thinkin' thoughts
   Of nothin' much but bed;
   When out o' nowhere, full of booze,
   Come roarin' Mister Clarence Cooze,
   Toward the fateful meetin'
   With the middle-class Mildred.

Oh Clarence, hey watch yourself boy, steady
May be too late already, Clarence.

5. With squealin' brakes and screamin' tires
   Clarence slowed to sixty,
   When he spotted Mildred
   Sittin' tired on a bale o' hay.
   "Can I ride you, ma'am, or take you to town,"
   Clarence asked politely;
   "I've hurt my ankle, help me down,"
   Is what he heard her say.

Oh Mildred, shame on you for lyin',
(What you're sellin' he's buyin', Mildred.)

6. Before her sneakers hit the ground
   Mildred grabbed his center.
   His eyes lit up, his fly slid down,
   Her middle class was spread:

Now he was not so rude
As to refuse her plea to enter,
And as he did he heard these words
(Which were the ones she said):

7. "Oh Clarence, Oh Clarence
Ain't had much lovin'
For almost a year,
An out o' work man's good for nothin'
But drinkin' and pissin' beer;
So treat me rough, stuff me, Clarence
Give me thrills, fill me, Clarence
Hey trashy daddy, open your throttle wide."

Oh Clarence, if you had heard my warnin'
You'd be sleeping late this mornin', Clarence.

8. For along the road come Vernon,
Returnin' home from Bertha's,
Feelin' kind o' mean that night
(Or so I've heard folks say.)
Well when Mildred see'd him, "Rape!" she
cried,
"Kill him," and Vernon would o' tried,
But luckily his drinkin' pal was Sheriff Billy
Shay.

9. They got him on illicit
Carnal knowledge of a woman;
That's worth thirty years
And that's where Clarence is today—
Doin' time at Folsom (where they learn you
to be wholesome)
And Mildred's home with Vernon and their
little baby Ray.

Oh Clarence, be glad you didn't hang:
That's what you get for messin' round with
middle-class poontang.

END

Rock Garden

The lights come up on a bare stage except for a couch downstage left and a chair upstage right. THE MAN *sits on the couch.* THE BOY *sits in the chair facing upstage, with his back to* THE MAN. THE BOY *never turns to address* THE MAN *but delivers all his lines into the air. They are both dressed in underwear. There is a long pause as the two just sit in their places. Saturday afternoon—just after lunch just before the ball game.*

MAN: It's uh—the lawn doesn't seem too bad this time of year.

A long pause.

Except around the sprinkler heads. It's always wet around the sprinkler heads so it grows all the time, I guess.

A long pause.

It's harder to mow around them too, I guess. It's hard to get the lawn mower in there close, I guess. It's pretty hard to get it in there close so it cuts, I guess.

A long pause.

The other house wasn't as bad as this one, was it? I mean the lawn wasn't. I mean the way the lawn was at the other place made it easier, I guess. I mean not

99

the lawn itself but more the way it was. You know?
The way it was just there. I mean it was just a square
piece of lawn. You know? It wasn't the lawn so much
as the way it was.

A long pause.

If we can get the fence painted by next week it
would be nice. You know? It's not a good fence but
if we could get it painted by next week it would be
nice I guess.

A long pause.

It needs to be saturated you know? That way it will
last. I remember the last one didn't last at all. You
remember the last one the way it fell down all the
time? But if it had been saturated it wouldn't have
fallen down at all. You know?

A long pause.

There's a new kind of preservative you can buy that
will be good for it. It only takes a couple coats. Yes,
just a couple will do it. White would be good. Sure.
Maybe a kind of off white. You know? What about a
kind of off white? You know what I mean? A kind
of different white. You know? Just a little different.
Not too much different from the way it is now. What
do you think? A different kind of white. You know?
So it won't be too much the same. It could be almost
the same but still be a little different. You know?

A long pause.

It would be fun I think. And what about the rock
garden? It's not bad for my never having made one
before. It's one of those new kinds. You know? With
rocks and stuff in it. It has a lot of rocks and stuff
from the trip. We found afterwards that it was really
worth carrying all those rocks around. You know?
It's a nice rock garden. It gives me something to do.
It keeps me pretty busy. You know? It feels good to
get out in it and work and move the rocks around
and stuff. You know. It's a good feeling. I change it
every day. It keeps me busy.

A long pause.

The orchard is the thing that really needs work. You know? It needs more work than the garden probably. It needs to be taken care of. It needs more water than it's been getting. You know what I mean? The new trees especially. They get brown pretty easily in this warm weather. I guess we should really take care of the orchard first. You know? This whole place will be looking like a new place. A new place. One of those new places with rock gardens all over and fountains. You know? You come up the street and there'd be a nice green lawn with a lot of rock gardens, and the irrigation running and the new trees all—all sort of green. You know? And the fence all painted with a different kind of white paint and the grass cut around the sprinkler heads and all that. You know?

101

A long pause.

BOY: When I come it's like a river. It's all over the bed and the sheets and everything. You know? I mean a short vagina gives me security. I can't help it. I like to feel like I'm really turning a girl on. It's a much better screw is what it amounts to. I mean if a girl has a really small vagina it's really better to go in from behind. You know? I mean she can sit with her legs together and you can sit facing her. You know? But that's different. It's a different kind of thing. You can do it standing, you know? Just by backing her up, you know? You just stand and she goes down and down until she's almost sitting on your dick. You know what I mean? She'll come a hundred times and you just stand there holding onto it. That way you don't even have to undress. You know? I mean she may not even want to undress at all. I like to undress myself but some girls just don't want to. I like going down on girls too. You know what I mean? She gives me some head and then I give her some. Just sort of a give and take thing. You know? The thing with a big vagina is that there isn't as much contact. There isn't as much friction. I mean you can move around inside her. There's different ways of ejaculation. I mean the leading up to it can be different. You can rotate motions. Actually girls really like fingers almost as well as a penis. You know. If you move your fingers fast enough they'd rather have it that way almost. I learned to use my thumb you know? You can get your thumb in much farther actually. I mean the thumb can go almost eight inches whereas a finger goes only five or six. You know? I don't know. I really like to come almost out and then go all the way into the womb. You know, very slowly. Just come down to the end and all the way back in and hold it. You know what I mean?

THE MAN *falls off the couch, the lights black out.*

END

Who: Whom

MAN *is discovered center stage in armchair, relaxed, legs crossed. To his right: a Victorian chaise longue, upholstered in leather. He lights a cigarette. As he does so* GIRL A *enters right. She is dressed like a Victorian parlor maid—black dress, high button shoes, maid's cap. She carries a birch rod.* MAN *watches her as she crosses to the chaise longue and kneels on it, placing the birch rod near her feet. She bends forward, resting her head on her folded arms. She raises her skirt and tucks it above her waist. She is wearing Victorian drawers. Her rear faces the audience as she bends again.* MAN *exhales, still watching her.* GIRL B *is now lowered from the flies, slightly to the left of* MAN. *She is encased in a net of stout rope, which dangles five feet above stage level. She is wearing a bikini. Her wrists and ankles are tied, her mouth is gagged, and she is doubled up.* MAN *watches her descent with impassive interest. Rising, he taps the ash from his cigarette and addresses the audience.*

MAN (*easy, slow, conversational tone*): Like most civilized people, I believe in democracy. I thought I'd better make that clear right from the beginning. I don't believe that any one person is essentially more important than any other. Or less. On the other hand, there are obviously differences between people. Some are taller or thinner or more redheaded than others. And some are what you might call more resonant.

105

He walks toward GIRL B.

For example, Susan here has resonance. I call her
Susan because that's the name of the character she is
playing. Susan is a pert English girl of good back-
ground, who has been captured and trussed up by a
tribe of savages in Sumatra. Indignities of many kinds
—some nameless, others specific—are in store for
her. Susan has resonance because many people respond to her. They love reading books about her, or
looking at pictures of her, or seeing films about her.
From time to time she's trussed up by Martians or
Vikings or Gauleiters. But she's always the same old
Susan, always defenseless, always known to her ad-
mirers as a damsel in distress. And she strikes a

chord. Can you hear it? (*Pause.*) It's a statistical fact that some of you can. That makes Susan a resounding person. Let's hope it comforts her in bondage—against which (GIRL B *wriggles desperately*) she struggles in vain.

He walks over to GIRL A.

This is Jean. Jean also has resonance. She is a parlor maid employed in a Scottish mansion during the middle years of the nineteenth century. The master of the house is an attractive widower, brushed with gray at the temples, and his regime is stern but just, like the glint in his ice-blue eyes. Jean has been caught stealing bottled plums, and now awaits chastisement at the hands of her master. She will now formally present herself.

GIRL A *pulls down her drawers to mid-thigh.*

She will now arch and offer.

GIRL A *arches her back. Jean is now fully disclosed. From between her buttocks, the puckered rim of a virgin target tremulously peeps.*

Like Susan, she is known in many disguises—as a wayward novice in an Irish cloister, or an indolent prefect at a strict finishing school. Many thousands of people respond to her plight, often quite vividly. Let us not blink the facts. A high degree of resonance attaches to Jean. May it solace her in her humility, that lovely, well-built girl.

He takes up a position between the two girls.

Remember Lenin—the great Lenin—who said that the world was divided into the "who" and "whom"? He was talking about those who do, and those to whom it is done. Wouldn't you say that Susan and Jean, in their very different ways, were a classic pair of whom?

He turns and stubs out his cigarette. He then faces the audience again.

You'll have noticed I said they were different. But how do they differ? In my view very significantly.

107

He indicates GIRL B.

Have a good squint at Susan. This girl is where she is as a direct consequence of physical coercion. Brute force and nimble fingers have been at work. The principle of choice—the very heartland of liberty— has been rudely violated. It's an outrage to the human spirit.

He turns to GIRL A.

Now let's take another look at Jean. She kneels there —or squats there—in a posture that must be profoundly embarrassing. You might even call it humiliating. However, if the spirit moves her, she is at liberty to get up and go. Jean, the submissive household servant in temporary disgrace, is a free agent.

He picks up the birch rod and fingers it.

And she is free not only as a parlor maid but as a human being. The girl you are watching—the docile squatter—is Eleanor Bron. (*Or whatever her real name is.*) Born 1941, trained at R.A.D.A., professional debut with Oldham Rep—you can see the details in the program. If Miss Bron, the employed female performer, decides now—tonight, this moment—to get up and leave the stage, there will be no reprisals. Neither I, nor the author, nor the director will hold it against her. She will return to the theater tomorrow night with her professional reputation untarnished. Whatever happens, she is the master of her fate.

He turns toward GIRL B.

Susan, for all her resonance, is dependent on the will of others. (*He shouts at the wings:*) Take Susan away! Whereas Eleanor—aged 25, divorced with one daughter, favorite food lobster chop suey—remains her own mistress. She is free to stop blushing and go.

He moves closer to her.

Are you listening to me, Eleanor?

She does not move.

Eleanor—do you want to leave the stage?

She does not move.

For the last time, will you please make a sign if you wish to leave the stage?

She does not move. Pause.

As I was saying, I am a strict believer in democracy.

SLOW FADE TO BLACKOUT

Four in Hand

Four chairs, backs to audience. Facing them, a large projection screen divided into four sections, one for each chair. Three men impatiently waiting. A doorbell rings.

1: There he is now. I told you he'd make it. (*He opens door.*)

GEORGE *enters: he wears a fedora.*

If you're going to join the group, George, you have to remember we always start on time.

GEORGE: Sorry I'm late, fellas.

2: We don't like people breakin' the rules, George.

GEORGE: I already said I'm sorry.

3: Look—We gonna talk, or we gonna jerk off?

1: O.K., let's get started. This is your seat, George. Now this (*pointing to screen*) is a new kind of machine— a telepathic thought transmitter. Whatever you think about flashes on the screen. Now the rules of the game are this: all of us think of things to jerk off to —until somebody comes—and the first guy who comes has to stop everybody else from coming. Got it?

GEORGE: Got it.

1: All right. Let's give it a try. Whatever comes to mind, George.

1 goes to his seat. GEORGE *sits between 2 and 3. Rhythmic music starts. Images start to flash rhyth-*

111

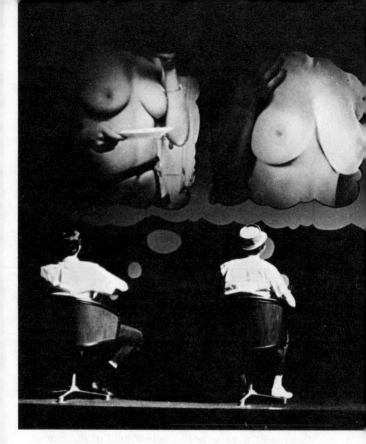

mically on the screens. The men's arms start to move
rhythmically in front of them. The screens facing 1,
2, and 3 show Hollywood and Playboy-type pinups.
GEORGE'S screen remains blank. The rhythm builds up
while screens 1, 2, and 3 are all pulsating with glam-
orous women. Suddenly, we hear the strains of the
"William Tell Overture", and during a crash of cym-
bals a picture of the Lone Ranger flashes on GEORGE'S
screen. All screens go blank and all four men stop
masturbating.
3: What the fuck was that?

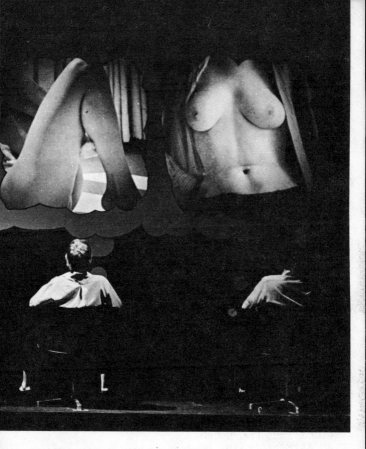

1: What are ya tryin' to do, George?

GEORGE: What's wrong?

2 (*rises, adjusting his pants*): I told you not to invite outsiders.

GEORGE: I'm sorry, fellas, it's the first thing that came into my mind.

2: We haven't had a vacancy in six months, George! Harvey only left because he got a divorce.

3: How'd you like a silver bullet up your ass?

1 (*walking to* GEORGE): You sure you're all right, George?

GEORGE: I'm fine, thanks.

1: All right, let's try it again.

They all sit down again.

And cut the horseshit, George.

The music starts again and the images start to flash. They are slightly more nude than before—close shots of breasts and bottoms. By trial and error, the four screens begin to form a composite picture. GEORGE is dutifully collaborating. Finally, at the height of the rhythm, screen facing 1 shows a nude model's head, screen facing 2 shows her breasts, screen facing 3 her legs. Pause. The recumbent image of the model is almost complete. Suddenly, the strains of the "William Tell Overture" again and another image of the Lone Ranger on GEORGE'S *screen.*

GEORGE (*exultantly*): Aha! A-a-a-a-ah!

He rises. His screen continues to flash the Lone Ranger. With one jabbing sweep of his arm he flashes Ranger pictures on the other screens as the music builds. As each image flashes, 1, 2, and 3 lose their concentration completely and give up the contest.

GEORGE (*turns as he goes to exit*): See you next week, fellas.

1: Get the fuck outta here!!!

Sound of four "whistling" gunshots as each remaining screen blacks out.

END

♋ Coming Together, Going Together

This piece is a reflection of the attitudes the actors had about auditioning for OH! CALCUTTA!; *about the rumors which were everywhere about what was going to be done in the show; and, in a capsule version, what the process of working on the show was like.*

It begins in darkness. The actors, in a semi-circle against the walls of the set, improvise single words which relate to their thoughts about OH! CALCUTTA! *before auditions.*

The lights come up, revealing this group "up against the wall."

BONI *and* KATIE *move down right, joined by* LEON *and* MARK. *The single words stop from the others. Quietly, hushed, they confess their feelings of inadequacy. They had not expected to be asked to sing as at a regular audition:*

MARK, LEON, KATIE,
BONI:
  I don't have a song
    to sing
  What should I do
  I don't have a song
    to sing
  Ooooooooooh
  What they'll want
    me to
  I'll do

Now the other actors interpolate thoughts as rumors, using only their voices—showing no emotion as the song continues:

MARGO: I hear all the guys in the show are gay.

117

I'll dance and sing

What the hell

I don't have a
   dance to dance

What will I do?

I don't have a
   dance to dance

Oooooooh.
What they'll want
   me to

I'll do.
I'll dance and sing.
What the hell?

I don't have a song
   to sing . . .
What the hell?

NANCY: I have to lose ten
pounds before I'll take off
my clothes.

BILL: I hear everybody's going to have to drop their
pants.

ALAN: What the hell, you do
it at home all the time.

RAINA: It's an Indian show
about sex.

A religious fuck show.

GEORGE: I'm out of shape.

NANCY: I hear the opening of
the show is all the guys
stand in a line and come
into the audience.

MARGO: I hear the cast al-
bum's going to be recorded
in the nude.

GEORGE: It's a lot of crap—
just to see everybody take
their clothes off.

*Now a group on the left comes together, a little
annoyed, more brazen, aggressive.* GEORGE, *joined by*
BILL, ALAN, *and* RAINA, *sings a hard talking blues:*

GEORGE: But I'm an
actor

There're some
things
I won't do.

In this Calcutta
show,

They're gonna want
you to screw,

Every night,

On cue.

Uh, uh, I didn't get
into show
Business just to
show my dick!
I mean,
What is the point?

ALAN:
I mean,
What does it prove?

BILL:
I mean,
The size of my
joint?   '

RAINA:
I mean,
The size of my
groove?

BILL: I hear they're gonna
measure the guys.

I swear to God, they're
gonna measure the guys.

ALAN: When they talk about
the size of your part, they
really mean it.

BILL: Who'd go up for a
small part?

BILL, ALAN, RAINA: Every
night?

On cue?

BONI: I'm out of shape.

119

ALL:
  I mean,
  Once you've seen
    one . . .

                              KATIE: Nudity is passe.

Now MARGO *and* NANCY, *in spotlight, move down and sing about their childhood dream of being a ballerina. Idealistic and innocent, they realize that there is much more freedom possible. The other two groups have remained together, talking and joking as actors do at auditions; sometimes the things they say become audible but there is no contact among the three groups.*

MARGO and NANCY:
  From the time I
    was little
  I wanted to be
  A ballerina.   BILL: I talk about pussy, but
                                I eat corned beef.
  And all I could see
  In the whole world
    to be
  Was ballerina.

                              BONI: Why do they call it
                                "Oh! Calcutta!"?
                              MARK: Well, they couldn't
                                call it "New Faces," could
                                they?

  And then I grew up
  And found there
    was
  More to life—
  Like acting and
    singing and
  Moving and being
    and
  Love and
  Life.

                              GEORGE: Who's the guy that's
                                going to have to fuck on
                                stage?

ALAN: Everybody's going to have to fuck on stage, but on alternate nights.

From the time I
    was little
I wanted to be
A ballerina.

LEON: No matter what we talk about, I get a hard-on.

And all I could see
In the whole world
    to be
Was ballerina.

MARK: What's that got to do with the wisdom of the East?

And then I grew up
And found there
    was
More to life—

RAINA: My parents expect it from this generation.

Like acting and
    singing and
Moving and being
    and
Love and
Life.

BONI: I think you'd look better without your clothes on.

BILL: If I can get through this, I can get through anything.

Now the three groups begin to move downstage in a line, singing their songs. Each actor is on his own, selling in the old "show biz" tradition. They are "on" —socking it to the audience. This is their big moment:

MARGO *and* NANCY:
> From the time I was little
> I wanted to be
> A ballerina.

MARK, LEON, KATIE, BONI:
> I don't have a song
> To sing.

BILL, ALAN, RAINA, GEORGE:
> But I'm an actor—

The three groups now sing simultaneously:

MARGO *and* NANCY:
> And all I could see
> In the whole world to be
> Was ballerina.
> O-h-h-h-h!

MARK, LEON, KATIE, BONI:
> What should I do?
> Oh! What they'll
> Want me to do, I'll do
> I'll dance and sing
> And. . .
> O-h-h-h-h!

BILL, ALAN, RAINA, GEORGE:
> There's some things I won't do—
> Oh! They're gonna want me
> To screw
> Every night!
> On stage!
> On cue!
> O-h-h-h-h!

VOICE FROM THE PIT *(blues rock shout)*:
> Well, I wasn't sure before
> But now I want it!

The actors stop, uncertain. The blues shout goes on. It becomes a rallying cry, and the actors get with it. They back away, leaving MARGO in the center. She strips, joyously throwing off her clothes; then she is joined by one actor at a time until all are naked,

dancing wildly to the blues rock. The actors are not in contact with one another but are having a great time.

> Well, I didn't know it was there
> But now I want it!
> I don't care what you say
> I'm gonna do it anyway because
> I want it.
>
> Yeah, I want it!
> Yeah, I want it!
> Yeah, I want it!
> Yeah, I want it!
> I don't care what you say
> I'm gonna do it anyway because
> I want it!
> I want it
> I want it!
> Want, Want, Want, Want, Want, Want, Want,
>   Want, Want it!
>
> I don't care what you say
> I'm gonna do it anyway because

> I want it!
> Want it!
> Want it!
> Want it!

Without warning, the music stops. Silence. The actors freeze—like statues caught in whatever movement they were making. Quiet, impressionist piano music. They speak: improvisations mirroring what the audience is thinking, what its attitudes might be. The actors hold their freeze while they speak. Examples:

What the fuck are they doing up there?

Looks like the perfect summer job.

There's a girl with a two-toned bird.

What do the men do when they get erections?

There's a lady in the first row with binoculars.

My God, that's my daughter up there.

All the men are circumsized. Must be a Jewish show.

Then let's go to Ratner's for supper.

When do you think they'll raid the joint?

I wonder what the cast parties are like.

The music stops. MARGO *begins to move silently, slowly, gracefully. The other actors are still talking. As she nears each actor, she brings him "to life"— the actors become silent as soon as they move, and they begin to explore the shape of one another's bodies, gracefully extending their own bodies in slow sways, reaching out to one another. But no one touches. Hands move over bodies and faces, only an inch from touching. As the tensions of not touching continue, the group contracts toward the center and begins reaching up as if to touch something above them. Now their bodies mass together—skin against skin—their hands all reaching upward. We hear the heavy breathing, the gasping of the actors. Then once more the rallying cry from the pit:*

> Well, I came here on a dare
> But now I want it!

The group explodes joyously now, touching, holding, swinging each other around. Something has broken open. While they jump and shout a line is being formed upstage. Finally, all the actors join in a line— a "daisy chain"—belly to belly, back to belly, back to back, humping in rhythm to the blues rock, yelling with the singer:

> I WANT IT!
> WANT IT!
> WANT IT!
> WANT IT!

BLACKOUT

Bang Bang, You're Almost Dead!

A typical American living room set. An extremely old couple, PETE and ELLA MCFADDEN, is seated. A younger couple, BOB and CAROL JORDAN, is about to leave.

MRS. JORDAN: Now, little Toby has a fever, Mom . . . so if she cries . . . give her some of the children's aspirin.

MR. JORDAN: Sorry you have to babysit for the third time this week . . . but we really appreciate it.

PETE (*very old and doddering*): Don't you worry, Bob . . . we'll take care of the little tykes.

BOB and CAROL exit. There is a pause as ELLA continues to mend a hole in her shawl. PETE slowly moves his jaws up and down, getting ready to insert his pipe. CAROL pops her head back in the door.

CAROL: Don't forget, if you need us . . . we'll be at the Kate Smith Fashion Show at the Municipal Auditorium. (*She exits.*)

This time ELLA gets up and does a comically slow walk to the window. She peers between the venetian blinds. We hear a car drive off. ELLA then takes the venetian blind ropes and gives a morse code signal by opening and shutting the blinds in slow succession. Finished with this, she goes to another chair and seats herself. There is another pause and then we hear a slow, weak rap on the door. PETE gets up slowly and his feebleness causes him to fall on his face.

ELLA: That was a good fall, Pete.

PETE: Thank you.

He gets up and moves to the door. He opens it. Two very old couples enter. They are BUD *and* MARTHA HIGGINS *and* RALPH *and* MARY ARMSTRONG. BUD *is carrying a bag and* RALPH *has a cane. They all cross.* BUD *and* MARTHA *go to the couch,* RALPH *and* MARY *to two adjacent chairs.* PETE *returns to the couch and sits down. All ad lib greetings.* BUD *takes a bottle of wine out of the bag and unscrews the cap.*

BUD: Well, here's the old bottle of Thunderbird.

He takes a swig, wipes off the top, and then passes it to RALPH. *He nips it.*

RALPH: I hope that's what's been makin' my urine turn red.

The bottle is passed around.

MARY: Let's make our usual phone call.

PETE *takes the phone from a table near the couch.*

PETE: O.K. Let's make up the number.

ELLA: How about Trafalgar as the exchange?

PETE: O.K. (*He dials T-R.*)

MARY: Five.

PETE *dials this and each number as it is called.*

BUD: Eight.

MARTHA: Nine.

RALPH: Seven.

ELLA: Three.

PETE *finishes dialing. Listens for ringing; then, as someone answers, he speaks:*

PETE: Just a minute, please.

PETE *holds the phone up so each member of the group can file by. They line up for this.* ELLA *is first. She steps up to the phone.*

ELLA: Balls.

RALPH: Tits.
MARTHA: Prick.
BUD: Asshole.
MARY: Shit.
PETE: So long, you old Cocker.

He hangs up and they all laugh and clap. During this, BUD and MARY take another drag on the wine bottle.

ELLA: Well . . . time to get at it.
PETE: O.K. Everybody throw your Social Security card on the coffee table.

They all pull their Social Security cards from little pockets in their suits and dresses. They throw them on the coffee table. MARTHA then reaches over and mixes them up. This done, RALPH reaches in first. He pulls out a card.

RALPH: Hot dog. I got you, Ella.
MARTHA: Should be an interesting evening. I got you, Mary.
PETE: That leaves you and me, Bud. (PETE *goes to a lamp and turns a switch so the room becomes dimmer.*) O.K. Let the games begin.

Each one starts to remove his clothes as he goes to his partner. RALPH goes to ELLA and they get on the floor. MARY and MARTHA also start to remove their clothes and get on the couch. BUD and PETE, removing their clothes, get on a chair together.

BUD: Be careful of my colostomy bag, Pete.
RALPH: Help me unsnap my truss.

Now, in the half-light, the various pairs slowly and feebly attempt various sexual maneuvers, gasping for breath, giving forth old sighs of sexual gratification.

MARY: I swear you're getting more wrinkles on your body every day. It's like screwing a prune.
PETE: Let me chew on your garter belt, Ella. It's the only thing that makes me horny.
MARTHA: I wouldn't mind dying right now. I can't wait for God's review of this.
ELLA: I don't think you're gonna get hard, Ralph.

131

Better go get the cane.

MARY: You know my fetish, Martha. Would you mind putting this radish in there?

ELLA (*hollering out from under* RALPH *on the floor, to* PETE *on the chair*): See if you can stretch it over, Pete. I have an insane desire to suck your foot.

PETE (*who is necking with* BUD): Here.

He extends his foot and ELLA *starts sucking it.*

BUD: Now, Pete, now. Snap the amyl nitrate under my nose.

A little five-year-old boy, JIMMY, *wearing Doctor Dentons, comes into the living room about six feet and stops.*

JIMMY (*sleepily*): I want a glass of water.

ELLA (*somewhat muffled from under* RALPH): Go back to bed, Jimmy! I'll give you eight glasses of water tomorrow.

MARTHA: My God. I actually just shit.

PETE: Go back to bed Jimmy or I'll kick your teeth in.

JIMMY *starts to exit.*

JIMMY: O.K. God bless you, Granpaw. (*He exits.*)

MARY: You know, the little fella resembles you, Pete.

ELLA: Yeah. Same size pecker.

All laugh. During the laugh, the phone rings. PETE *gets up from the chair and crosses over to answer.*

BUD: I wonder who the hell that is.

PETE: Probably the Pope calling to tell us to lay off.

RALPH: Don't worry, Cardinal Cushing will be on our side.

PETE *picks up the phone.*

PETE: Oh, hi Carol . . . (*Pause.*) Oh everything's quiet here. Jimmy had a bad dream . . . but we sent him back to bed. (*Pause.*) What? You're coming right home? ! ! ! (*He covers the phone mouthpiece. To the others:*)—The fashion show's dull and she's worried about Toby's fever. (*Back to phone.*) There's really nothing to worry about. But if it'll ease your mind, we'll see you.

He hangs up the phone and quickly turns the lights up to bright.

Move your asses everybody . . . they'll be home right away.

Now follows a mad rush while the old people try to get their clothes back on. Some people get into the wrong clothes, the wrong shoes, etc. People fall over one another.

MARY: Who's got my surgical bra?

RALPH: I always smoke after sex. Do I have time?

ELLA: No, you asshole. Everybody get out of here and finish dressing in the car.

They all start to exit, grabbing clothes as they go.

BUD: See ya next Thursday . . . we'll be sitting with the Conway children.

MARTHA: Don't they have a sauna?

PETE: Never mind. Get out of here.

He pushes them out and closes the door behind them.
PETE and ELLA straighten up as best they can and go to the couch.

PETE (*on his cross to couch*): Bud was quite good tonight.

ELLA (*on her cross*): Ralph was a little soggy.

They hear someone at the door and they feign sleep.
MR. and MRS. JORDAN enter.

CAROL: Aw, look, Bob, they've fallen asleep already. They look so saintly sitting there.

BOB: Yeah . . . but it's kind of sad. The poor bastards never have any fun.

BLACKOUT

I'll Shoot Your Dog If You Don't

Night. What looks to be a prison cell. A room, bare except for a single bed and the figure sleeping in it. The counterpane is white, the bed iron. There is a dress carefully laid out on the end of the bed facing the audience. It is a severe black dress. Hanging from one post of the bed is a flimsy brassiere, and from the other, knickers suggesting an equally frivolous taste. There are a pair of tights to one side of the dress. It is obvious that they have had air blown into them because they have the consistency of legs. A door leads to a passage where there is a faint light. A man enters the passage. He is dressed in a black gown and is wearing a barrister's wig. He is smoking a cigar and carrying a long flashlight. He stands in the passage and looks through the observation hole, then he throws the cigar away, enters the room on tiptoe, crosses to the bed and flicks the flashlight on and off to arrest the sleeping figure. A young girl sits up looking startled. He talks in a whisper.

HIM: Remember me?

HER (*very frightened*): Who is it?

HIM: Me. Counsel.

HER: What's wrong? What's the matter?

HIM: Nothing. I just happened to be going by.

A GUARD *walks down the passage. We see him. They hear him. The girl opens her mouth and catches her breath in terror. The* GUARD *does not look through the*

135

observation hole. As his footsteps fade she speaks.

HER: That was the guard. Must have been.

HIM: It doesn't matter, I'm Counsel. I'm privileged. *(He is walking around the room sniffing.)*

HER: How is my dog?

HIM *(in answer to his own sniff)*: Insecticide?

HER: Toilet water.

HIM: Smells like insecticide to me. *(Pointing to the stockings.)* That stocking's not right; you know I like a fat leg.

HER: Does my dog whine?

HIM *(abruptly)*: Come on, get up. We have business to discuss.

The girl leans forward and takes her brassiere and knickers from the bedpost. She slips the straps of her nightdress down very warily and as she puts on the brassiere she bends right forward until her head touches her knees. She then makes rather a ceremony of getting her knickers on without taking her feet out of the covers. All the time while she is doing this he has his back to her and is addressing himself to the tights. He touches the heel, the blown-out calf, the knee of each leg, and lastly the crotch. He murmurs to them. He uses the flashlight to see them by because the light on the stage is dim throughout. She puts the dress on while still in her bed and when she stands on the floor it is indeed the virginal attire that she presents. She whistles lightly to let him know that she is dressed. He turns around and says rather pretentiously:

HIM: I had a very substantial supper. I had to have exercise.

HER: I touch my toes fifty-three times morning and night.

HIM: I bet you do.

His voice is hearty and full of sexual innuendo. She is timid and respectful, too respectful. All her movements are modest and careful; for instance, she puts her hand to her throat and raises her collar that little bit higher, she pulls down the cuffs of her dress, she locks her hands, symbols of chastity.

HIM: I had eels, as a matter of fact.

HER: Is that the fish that wiggles?

HIM: You know nothing.

She starts to draw the covers up over the bed and then to tuck them in at the sides.

Which is part of your charm.

HER: Does my dog go for a stroll in the evening? To meet another dog?

He sits on the bed. She sits on the bed, but a distance away.

HIM: He licks himself.

HER: I hope you know he's called Boris.

HIM: I was going over your file this afternoon and do you know what occurred to me? (*Pause.*) What you've done with all those trinkets, all those things you stole, earrings, pearls, studs, stones, precious *and* semiprecious.

HER: Gave them to my friends.

He smiles, he sighs, he moves closer.

HIM: Yes! A woman always gives.

He takes off his wig and then his gown.

It has been bothering me all day. To know what you did with them, with your trinkets.

He takes her hands and applies them to opening the buttons of his shirt. She does this without looking at him. The flashlight, which is alight, lies between them on the bed.

HER: Where does this get us?

HIM: Closer, I hope.

HER: I mean, my case.

HIM (*very formal*): The discussions will continue on appropriate and necessary levels until the issues have been resolved. (*Pause. Suggestive voice.*) I had a brainwave.

HER (*sitting up tensely*): What was that?

HIM: That you still have one or two . . .

HER (*quickly*): What? Where?

137

HIM: Somewhere (*he touches her body with quick deft movements*) in your possession.

She is shaking her head to convince him of her innocence.

They say theft is erotic.

HER: What's that?

HIM: Eechy weechy whoo.

HER: Uh-uh, eechy weechy whoo.

He takes the flashlight and trains it on her body.

HIM: You're asking for trouble you know, having a little trinket like that.

He uses the flashlight to look into her ears, her nose, her mouth, under the neckline of her dress.

Nothing there. Small throughout. Luckily they're a good color.

While he is talking she puts her hand under her own dress and takes a button from her belly button. She hands it to him.

HER: It's mother-of-pearl.

HIM: Got any others?

HER: Might have.

HIM: Things are beginning to happen.

HER: To who?

HIM: To us. To you and to me, to me and to you.

HER: I hope you're not going to start anything.

She is about to back away from him but it is too late. With one hand he opens her mouth very wide and with the other he forces the flashlight in.

HIM: Got your washing machine on?

She mumbles but cannot be understood because the flashlight is in her mouth and impedes her speech. He moves the flashlight around and around very rapidly.

Now no biting.

Use your tongue.

That's it, salivate.

A little refreshment.

A lasting lather.

That's better, that's the idea.

Thinking of breeches.

He stands up and picks her off the bed and she now holds the flashlight of her own accord. He puts her kneeling on the floor. He sits on the bed so that he is level with her. He tears open his trousers. He takes the flashlight from her mouth and throws it a distance away.

New improved.
See inside . . .
Made to a special formula that
   clings to the sides,
Right round the S bend,
Different materials make a different
   impact, eh?

Squish, squash,
Ah, the adulteress.
Look at me, slut.
Nice times you're having.

The GUARD watches from the corridor. On stage for a moment there is nothing but the panting of the couple. At the very height of this he rises and clicks on a bedside light which has a lampshade round it. In contrast with the darkness the place is ugly and brutal. She rises and walks away from the audience. Her dress, brassiere, and knickers are in a heap on the floor. As he stands up to rebutton his trousers he kicks her clothes out of his way. It is with a strident voice that she addresses him.

HER: Listen mate, I told you yesterday. Get another flashlight will you, this one stinks.

HIM: I must ask you not to address me like that. Remember our roles.

She puts on her nightdress and then goes to the end of the bed where she lays her dress carefully, hangs up the brassiere, hangs the knickers. As he exits with his large unlit flashlight, the GUARD enters with his long black baton, obviously to repeat the ritual. She has gotten into bed and is lying very quietly.

END

St. Dominic's, 1917

GWEN, FAUVETTE, MORVYTH: *Fifth Form Girls*
ELSPETH: *Fifth Form Monitor*
MISS BEESLEY: *Headmistress*

Drop-cloth of covers of girls' school books circa 1917. Recorded sound of girls singing school song. Superimpose projection caption: "THE FIFTH FORM AT ST. DOMINIC'S, 1917." *Fade caption. Superimpose second caption:* "CHAPTER ONE." *Fade caption. Superimpose third caption:* "GWEN MAKES A BAD START." *Meanwhile, over the public address system:*

VOICE (*female*): "In the depth of every Englishman's subconscious, there is a cat-of-nine-tails and a schoolgirl in black stockings." Remark attributed to the French humorist, Pierre Daninos.

The school song, which has faded for the announcement, swells up and ends. The drop-cloth rises. Behind it are three dormitory camp beds, occupied by GWEN, FAUVETTE, *and* MORVYTH. *A bell rings.* ELSPETH, *the dormitory prefect, enters, dressed in school uniform—gymslip, black stockings, white blouse, and school tie.*

ELSPETH: Come on, girls! Stir your old bones! Don't want to treat you to a jaw-wag on the first day of term. Let's have no monkey tricks, or Miss Beesley'll be down on us like a ton of bricks!

GWEN (*sitting up in bed*): Must you be so jinky,

Elspeth? This child's fagged out entirely!

ELSPETH: Stop frivolling, you silly young blighter, or I'll spliflicate you!

FAUVETTE (*to audience*): Fumed Elspeth.

GWEN: You needn't be so peacocky, just because you're a monitor!

FAUVETTE (*to audience*): Chirruped Gwen, with a grin on her impish face.

ELSPETH (*to* GWEN): Now listen to me, you young scalliwag. You may have been the firebrand of the Fourth, but this is your first day in the Fifth, and you'll have a grizzly time of it unless you mind your manners!

GWEN (*jumping out of bed and slipping dark blue knickers under her nightie*): No use expecting me to knuckle under, Elspeth, I'm as used to scolding as eels to skinning!

ELSPETH: Any more chat from you, and I'll report you to Miss Beesley. And a summons from that worthy rarely bodes good fortune to the recipient. (*To audience.*) Gwen's gauche and brusque, but at heart she's unimpeachable!

MORVYTH, *still curled up in bed, suddenly bursts into tears.*

(*going to* MORVYTH'S *bed.*) Hello! Whence this thusness? Gracious, girl, turn off the waterworks! We don't care for this sickly sort of stuff at St. Dominic's.

MORVYTH: I'm sorry, Elspeth, but I'm dreadfully homesick!

FAUVETTE (*to audience. By now she is languidly dressing and washing*): Wailed Morvyth.

ELSPETH: For goodness' sake bottle it up, Morvyth!

MORVYTH: But my brother's volunteered to be a Tommy, you see, and they're sending him out to the front!

ELSPETH: Then you ought to be proud of him, you silly goose! I've met some of the lads who've come back blinded from the war, and they're twice as cheerful and patient as you.

MORVYTH (*hugging* ELSPETH): You are a trump, Elspeth!

ELSPETH (*extricating herself*): Don't, Morvyth!

FAUVETTE (*to audience*): Said Elspeth huskily.

ELSPETH (*to audience*): Morvyth is a dear, delightful, lovable lazybones, with sweetly coaxing little ways, and a helpless confiding look in her blue eyes. Her fossils form the nucleus of the school museum.

All the girls are now out of bed and dressing. They follow the same procedure: having pulled on their knickers, they remove their nighties and put on white blouses, gymslips, school ties, and black stockings held by garters.

GWEN (*to audience*): The spiciest character in the form is Fauvette, otherwise known as "The Kipper," and rumored to be the richest girl in school.

FAUVETTE (*to audience*): Some of the girls are fearfully down on me because my wealthy parents send me postal orders. They tease me and call me "Proudie" or "Madam Conceit."

Bell rings.

ELSPETH: Oops! Two minutes to go before Assembly. Scooterons-nous this very sec! I'll nip ahead. Fauvette, I'm counting on you to see to it that the Fifth is there on time in full fig! (ELSPETH *exits.*)

FAUVETTE: *Strafe* the dear old Fifth as far as I'm concerned! Elspeth may be in a rush, but it's not this child's usual way of proceeding!

GWEN: Fauvette!

FAUVETTE (*to audience*): Interposed Gwen, her dark eyes dancing.

GWEN: Will the Bumble Bee be taking us for English composition?

All three, fully dressed, have come downstage. The drop-cloth falls behind them.

FAUVETTE: The Bumble Bee? Great Minerva, how ignorant the new bug is! My poor babe, let me initiate you into the shibboleths of the Fifth. Be it known to you that our respected Head, Miss Beesley, vulgarly known as the Bumble Bee, is among our elect set yclept Lemonade—partly owing to her habit of fizzing over, and partly owing to a certain acid quality in her temper.

GWEN: But why shouldn't I call her the Bumble Bee if I want to?

FAUVETTE: Because, old sport, you mustn't correct your betters.

GWEN: And what makes you better than I am?

MORVYTH (*to audience*): Sniffed Gwen in her forthright way.

FAUVETTE: Because, frabjous child, your parents are humble folk, whereas mine are bearing the nation's burdens on their shoulders.

MORVYTH: Do stow it, Fauvette!

FAUVETTE (*to* GWEN): Make no mistake, I shall take care to keep my weekly postal order locked up in my desk, in case you snaffle it!

GWEN: I wouldn't touch anything of yours with a pair of tongs!

MORVYTH (*to audience*): Flared Gwen.

FAUVETTE: And I wouldn't touch anything of yours *except* with a pair of tongs. You're so unwashed!

GWEN: You old bluebottle!

GWEN *throws herself on* FAUVETTE. *They pummel each other, rolling around the stage.* MORVYTH *looks aghast. Suddenly* ELSPETH *re-enters, looking fierce.*

ELSPETH (*separating the combatants*): Peace, turbulent herd! Fauvette, tell me what happened.

FAUVETTE: Please don't think me a rotten sneak, Elspeth, but Gwen set upon me!

GWEN (*hotly*): I say . . .

MORVYTH (*to audience*): Interjected Gwen.

ELSPETH: Did you start this imbroglio, Gwen?

GWEN: Great heavens, no, Fauvette egged me on!

ELSPETH: Then let me give you both a word of advice, my lofty Pharaohs! Pride frequently comes before a fall.

ELSPETH *seizes* GWEN *by the ear.* FAUVETTE *looks smug.*

MORYTH (*to audience*): I see breakers ahead.

All four girls freeze in this grouping.

VOICE (*female; over public address system*): You have now met Gwen, Fauvette, Morvyth, and Elspeth. At the end of this sketch, one of them will be publicly spanked. By a process of elimination, you, the audience, will decide on the victim. You can now eliminate either Gwen or Fauvette. Please indicate your choice by raising your right hand. Is it Gwen?

GWEN *steps forward from group and faces audience.*

Or Fauvette?

FAUVETTE *does the same.*

(*Using whichever name gets the most votes*)—is hereby exonerated.

Blackout

School song is heard again. Drop-cloth appears with projected caption: "HIGH JINKS AND HOT WATER IN THE OFFING." *Drop-cloth rises. Lights go up to reveal classroom with desks and blackboard.* FAUVETTE, GWEN, *and* MORVYTH *are seated, chattering.* ELSPETH *enters.*

ELSPETH: *Cave,* all concerned! Miss Beesley's approaching in full sail.

All sit demurely upright. MISS BEESLEY *enters in scholastic gown.*

MISS BEESLEY: Good morning, girls!

ALL: Good morning, Miss Beesley!

ELSPETH (*to audience*): Miss Beesley is a handsome and imposing woman with a stern cast of features.

MISS BEESLEY: Members of the Fifth! I have some remarks to address to two of your number. First of all, Morvyth.

MORVYTH *rises.*

It's come to my ears that you have been acting like a weeping cherub on a monument. Now that won't do at all—we've no patience with grousers at St. Dominic's. It's your bounden duty to be bubbling and girlish so that you can carry away happy memories

145

of your lighthearted schooldays when you go out into the world to be a woman. Do you understand, Morvyth?

MORVYTH: Yes, Miss Beesley, I'll do my uttermost. (*She sits.*)

MISS BEESLEY: There's a gallant girl. And now for the egregious madcap of the Fourth, lately translated to more august surroundings.

GWEN *ruefully rises. The other girls giggle.*

It's been brought to my attention that the afore-mentioned young scamp has celebrated her arrival in the Fifth by indulging in pugilistic practices with one of her senior bedfellows. Now Gwen, it's A.1 to be high-spirited, but if you overstep the mark again, there'll be a painful reckoning behind my green baize door. Compris?

GWEN (*flushed*): Oui—I mean, yes, Miss Beesley! (*She sits.*)

ELSPETH (*to audience*): It's an open secret that Miss Beesley, strict disciplinarian though she is, has a sneaking weakness for Gwen.

MORVYTH (*to audience*): "The Bumble Bee rows Gwen but she likes her," is the general verdict.

FAUVETTE *has meanwhile been rummaging through her desk.*

FAUVETTE: Miss Beesley!

MISS BEESLEY: What is it, child?

FAUVETTE: Somebody or other has nabbed my postal order! It's vanished from my desk!

MORVYTH: Great jumping Jehosephat!

Continue below if GWEN *has been eliminated earlier:*

FAUVETTE: And what's more, I told Morvyth only this morning that

Continue below if FAUVETTE *has been eliminated earlier:*

FAUVETTE: And what's more, I told Gwen only this morning that

I was going to put it
there.

Everyone stares at
MORVYTH *who looks
appalled.*

GWEN (*to audience*):
Morvyth stood aghast,
utterly dumbfounded
at the defalcation.
MORVYTH: Fauvette's a
fibber! She's just try-
ing to make me blub!

The four girls and
MISS BEESLEY *freeze
in a group.*

VOICE (*female; over pub-
lic adress system*):
Three girls are still
eligible for punish-
ment.

*The girls in question
step forward.*

In precisely four min-
utes, one of them will
be whipped. We now
invite you to eliminate
either Fauvette or
Morvyth. Please raise
your right hand if you
wish to spare Fauvette.
(*Pause for vote to be
noted.*) Or Morvyth.
(*Another pause.*)
———is hereby ex-
onerated.

I was going to put it
there!

Everyone stares at
GWEN, *who looks
appalled.*

MORVYTH (*to audience*):
Gwen stood aghast,
utterly dumbfounded
at the defalcation.
GWEN: I loathe pointing
the finger at a chum,
but you told Morvyth
as well as yours truly.

The four girls and
MISS BEESLEY *freeze
in a group.*

VOICE (*female; over pub-
lic adress system*):
Three girls are still
eligible for punish-
ment.

*The girls in question
step forward.*

In precisely four min-
utes, one of them will
be whipped. We now
invite you to eliminate
either Morvyth or
Gwen. Please raise
your right hand if
you wish to spare
Morvyth. (*Pause for
vote to be noted.*)
Or Gwen. (*Another
pause.*)———is here-
by exonerated.

Blackout

School song again. Drop-cloth appears with caption:
"A BEANO IN THE DORM AT WHICH A SCORE IS SET-
TLED." *Drop-cloth rises. Lights up to reveal dormitory setting as in the first scene. The four girls are
onstage, slipping out of gymslips and changing into
nighties. Other girls could also be present, already
wearing pyjamas, nightdresses, and other kinds of
schoolgirl deshabille.*

ELSPETH: Who's in favor of tripping the light fantastic
before we broach the ginger beer?

FAUVETTE: What a perfectly chubby wheeze!

GWEN: Absolutely slap-bang!

All the girls cheer.

ELSPETH: Right-ho! Combs and paper at the ready!
One-two-three!
*Some of the girls produce combs and paper and start
to play a popular waltz. The others choose partners
and dance.* ELSPETH *approaches* MORVYTH, *who looks
lonely.*

ELSPETH: Care to borrow my bedjacket, young Morvyth?

MORVYTH: You're a brick, Elspeth, but I'm not sure
that lilac's my color.

FAUVETTE (*to audience*): Mumbled Morvyth, turning
hot with pleasure at the bare idea.

ELSPETH: Never mind, baby, you look nice in anything.

FAUVETTE (*to audience*): Returned Elspeth soothingly.

ELSPETH: And your white petticoat's a perfect dream. I
always said it was a shame to hide it under a dress.
ELSPETH *and* MORVYTH *waltz together. The mood
and tempo are dreamy and romantic. Everyone except* FAUVETTE *and the comb-and-paper players are
dancing.*

FAUVETTE (*to audience*): Gwen's cheeks were scarlet
and Morvyth's long fair hair floated out picturesquely
as she twirled around in Elspeth Moseley's arms.

FAUVETTE *moves towards* GWEN'S *bed. Suddenly,*
MISS BEESLEY, *in a dressing gown, marches into the
dormitory.*

ALL: *Cave*—the Bumble Bee!

MISS BEESLEY (*genially*): I hope I'm not turning up like the proverbial bad penny! It's not my intention to be the specter at the feast. I was deeply impressed by your doughty efforts in the end-of-term exams, and I thought it might not be taken amiss if I put in an appearance at your beano.

The girls cheer.

Let the festivities continue.

ELSPETH: In honor of the Bumble Bee's—I mean Miss Beesley's—presence, may I propose a toast in foaming flagons of ginger pop! (*She offers* MISS BEESLEY *a glass.*) Here's to the health of St. Dominic's, the grandest school of all!

The girls all raise their glasses, but before they can drink, FAUVETTE *cries out:*

FAUVETTE: Just a jiffy, you fellows! I've found my postal order—and it's here, in Elspeth's locker.

General cry of astonishment. FAUVETTE *points at the locker.* ELSPETH *goes over and snatches the postal order from inside it.* GWEN *looks abashed. The girls freeze in a group.*

VOICE: Your final choice between Elspeth (ELSPETH *steps forward.*) . . . and Fauvette/Morvyth/Gwen. (*The other victim steps forward.*) Do you eliminate Elspeth? (*Pause for vote.*) Or Fauvette/Morvyth/Gwen? (*Pause for vote.*)———is hereby exonerated.

The group unfreezes and the action continues.

FAUVETTE: I hate being a tattle-tale, but her locker was open, and there it was!

MISS BEESLEY (*to* ELSPETH): Can you explain how Fauvette's postal order came to be in your locker?

ELSPETH: It's not an atom of use asking me, I haven't the ghost of a notion!

GWEN (*to audience*): Was any wretched girl ever in such a fix?

MISS BEESLEY: Things will go easier for you if you make a clean breast of it.

ELSPETH: I'm sorry, Miss Beesley, but I have nothing to confess.

GWEN (*to audience*): Hot tears came welling up, but Elspeth brushed them away angrily.

MISS BEESLEY: Theft is an ugly word, Elspeth. In all the years of my headmistressship, incidents such as this have very seldom occurred. I have had unruliness and disobedience before, but in the whole of my experience never a girl more brazen than you. It is of course impossible for me to allow you to remain at St. Dominic's.

Continue as follows if ELSPETH *is the victim:*

I will deal with you myself in the morning. In the meantime, I shall hand you over to the tender mercies of Gwen—the new monitor of the Fifth— who has full disciplinary powers. (*She exits.*)

GWEN (*to audience*): The Bumble Bee always reminds me of an ancient Roman— the State first and foremost in her estimates, and herself nowhere. (*She seats herself on one of the beds.*) Hairbrush if you please, Elspeth, or are you going to show the white feather?

Continue as follows if GWEN *is the victim:*

MISS BEESLEY *turns to leave. As she does so,* MORVYTH *rushes forward.*

MORVYTH: Please, Miss Beesley, may I speak?

MISS BEESLEY: What is it, Morvyth?

MORVYTH: I'll take my oath Elspeth's telling the truth. The real culprit is Gwen. She's green with envy because Elspeth's top dog and she'll go to any lengths to do her down. I saw her putting the postal order into Elspeth's locker!

MISS BEESLEY: Is this true, Gwen?

GWEN *is silent.*

Continue as follows if
MORVYTH *is the*
victim:

MISS BEESLEY *turns to leave. As she does so,* GWEN *rushes forward.*

GWEN: Please, Miss Beesley, may I speak?

MISS BEESLEY: What is it, Gwen?

GWEN: I'll take my oath Elspeth's telling the truth. The culprit is Morvyth. She's green with envy because Elspeth is top dog, and she'll go to any lengths to do her down. I saw her putting the postal order into Elspeth's locker.

MISS BEESLEY: Is this true, Morvyth?

MORVYTH *is silent.*

Continue as follows if
FAUVETTE *is the*
victim:

MISS BEESLEY *turns to leave. As she does so,* MORVYTH *rushes forward.*

MORVYTH: Please, Miss Beesley, may I speak?

MISS BEESLEY: What is it, Morvyth?

MORVYTH: I'll take my oath Elspeth's telling the truth. Fauvette's green with envy because Elspeth's top dog, and she'll go to any lengths to do her down. The real culprit is Fauvette herself! I saw her putting the postal order into Elspeth's locker.

MISS BEESLEY: Is this true, Fauvette?

FAUVETTE *is silent.*

ELSPETH: I may be a
blighter, but at least I
don't funk!

Are you willing to
swear that it's false?

GWEN *shakes her
head.*

In that case, I must
apologize to Elspeth,
who has undeservedly
borne the brunt of my
strictures. As for you,
Gwen, you have set a
most pernicious ex-
ample, and I will deal
with you myself in
the morning. In the
meanwhile, I shall
hand you over to the
tender mercies of your
monitor, who has full
disciplinary powers.
(*She exits.*)
GWEN (*to audience*):
The Bumble Bee al-
ways reminds me of
an ancient Roman—
the State first and
foremost in her esti-
mates, and herself
nowhere.
ELSPETH (*seating herself
on one of the beds*):
Hairbrush, if you
please, Gwen, or are
you going to show the
white feather?
GWEN: I may be a
blighter, but at least
I don't funk!

Are you willing to
swear that it's false?

MORVYTH *shakes her
head.*

In that case, I must
apologize to Elspeth,
who has undeservedly
borne the brunt of my
strictures. As for you,
Morvyth, you have set
the most pernicious
example, and I will
deal with you in the
morning. In the mean-
while, I shall hand
you over to the tender
mercies of your
monitor, who has full
disciplinary powers.
(*She exits.*)

GWEN (*to audience*):
The Bumble Bee al-
ways reminds me of
an ancient Roman—
the State first and
foremost in her esti-
mates, and herself
nowhere.

ELSPETH (*seating herself
on one of the beds*):
Hairbrush, if you
please, Morvyth, or
are you going to show
the white feather?

MORVYTH: I may be a
blighter, but at least I
don't funk.

Are you willing to
swear that it's false?

FAUVETTE *shakes her
head.*

In that case, I must
apologize to Elspeth,
who has undeservedly
borne the brunt of my
strictures. As for you,
Fauvette, you have
set a most pernicious
example, and I will
deal with you myself
in the morning. In the
meanwhile, I shall
hand you over to the
tender mercies of your
monitor, who has full
disciplinary powers.
(*She exits.*)

GWEN (*to audience*):
The Bumble Bee al-
ways reminds me of
an ancient Roman—
the State first and
foremost in her esti-
mates, and herself
nowhere.

ELSPETH (*seating herself
on one of the beds*):
Hairbrush, if you
please, Fauvette, or
are you going to show
the white feather?

FAUVETTE: I may be a
blighter, but at least
I don't funk!

The VICTIM *fetches a hairbrush from her washstand, gives it to the* MONITOR *and bends over her knee. The* MONITOR *slowly raises the* VICTIM'S *nightie to the waist and, even more slowly, pulls down her knickers. The other girls gather round to watch the spanking. It takes place in slow motion, with the* VICTIM *ritualistically wriggling as each blow falls. The girls count in unison. We should feel that this is a kind of tribal ceremony—the sacrifice of the willing victim. As the* MONITOR *spanks, it might be a good idea to project on the back-cloth a moving close shot of the* VICTIM'S *bottom. The counting grows louder and the pace increases. At about the count of ten, we hear electronic "take-off" music, possibly like the sound used by the Beatles in "A Day in the Life." As this sound and the spanking reach a climax, we*

BLACKOUT

 **Bath**

Interior of a small apartment. Stage right, a living room furnished in dark, overstuffed Victorian; center, a bathtub in a hallway, and off the hallway a john; left, a bedroom featuring a large brass bed, the head of which faces directly downstage so that were someone lying in it, only the top of the head would be visible. Dim lights are on in the living room. The rest is dark. Seated around a coffee table are a YOUNG MAN, *a* YOUNG WOMAN, *and a second* YOUNG WOMAN (WOMAN 2). *At rise, the three of them are laughing loudly, drinks in their hands, at a story the first* WOMAN *is telling.*

WOMAN: So there I was, in the middle of Central Park, trying to get this goddamn kite down out of the tree, see. And I'm halfway up the tree, and this little crowd—mostly guys—is gathered underneath me looking up and laughing their balls off. So I'm getting a little sore, you know? Not one of them would help. So finally I yell down at them: "Hey! Instead of standing around laughing like a bunch of dumb bastards, how about one of you giving me a hand?" And one of them yells up "I'll give you a hand, baby." And they all laugh again. Now another guy climbs up on the tree a ways, reaches up and pinches me in the ass. Then I realize I got no underwear on underneath. Well, it was too much! And I start laughing too. Now we're all laughing and they're standing down there looking up my kazoo.

All in gales of laughter, drinking.

MAN: What happened then?

WOMAN: Oh, nothing really. I mean, they were harmless, you know? I just finally got the kite down and we all laughed some more and they went away.

MAN: Great story.

WOMAN: Yeah, isn't it? I'm telling you, that moment when I realized I was bare-assed was really something. You want another drink?

MAN: O.K., fine.

WOMAN 2: Not for me. I think I'm gonna split.

WOMAN: Oh, really? You have to?

WOMAN 2: Yeah, well I've got to get up pretty early and make it to the unemployment office.

MAN: Listen, maybe I ought to go.

WOMAN: If you want to, fine, but you don't have to.

WOMAN 2: Listen, if it wasn't for the check thing I'd stay too. Don't let me break up the party.

WOMAN: Sure.

MAN: Well, O.K.

> WOMAN *gets up to pour him a drink, while* WOMAN 2 *puts her coat on. She goes to the door.*

WOMAN 2 (*to* MAN): It was real nice to have met you. (*To* WOMAN.) I'll give you a call tomorrow, like late afternoon.

WOMAN: Bye, sweetie.

> WOMAN 2 *exits. Moment of silence as the two sip their drinks.*

MAN (*He takes off his shoes conspicuously*): Oh. Feels good.

WOMAN: Great. Make yourself comfortable. She's really great.

MAN: Yes, she seems like a very nice person, but I'm not really sorry she had to leave.

WOMAN: Why?

MAN: Well, I was hoping we'd have a chance to be alone. You, uh, sort of turn me on.

WOMAN: Groovy! I love to turn people on! So does she. I mean, that's why it wouldn't have made any difference. Unless it would have to you.

MAN: No, no, of course not. I didn't realize that was, uh, the scene.

WOMAN: It's not a scene. Oh, shit! Let's forget it, O.K.?

MAN: Sure. Listen, maybe I should go.

WOMAN: Oh, don't be so jumpy, all right? I'd just like to get to know you a little. You seem like an interesting guy.

MAN: Sure.

WOMAN: Tonight isn't the first time I've seen you in Jimmie's. In fact, I think we were introduced once.

MAN: Yes. I was in one night with Lou and his wife and you came over to the table to say hello.

The lights are dimming.

WOMAN: Right. I really like it in there, sort of a nice crowd. It's a very warm atmosphere, you know? Really groovy. Especially on weekends.

By now the lights are black, the conversation fading with them. Lights come up on the two, still on the couch, now slumped, legs out on the coffee table.

MAN: Man, it must be about five o'clock.

WOMAN: I guess.

MAN: I, uh . . .

Pause. Neither moves. Then he moves to her and kisses her very tenderly.

WOMAN: Mmmmmmmmm. That was nice.

More kissing, tenderly, then with more passion. Touching. They are both digging it.

Hey, listen! I'd like to take a bath. You want to take a bath with me?

MAN: I'd like to go to bed with you.

WOMAN: Well, I think I'd like to go to bed with you, too, but I'm not sure I'd like to go to bed with you right now.

MAN: What does that mean?

WOMAN: It's not complicated. I dig you and all, but right at the moment I feel like taking a bath, and if you want to join me, you're welcome.

157

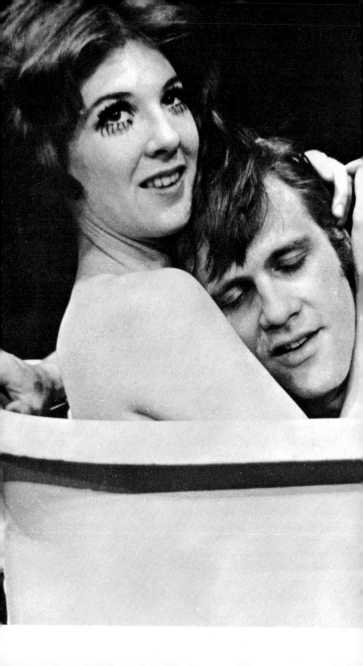

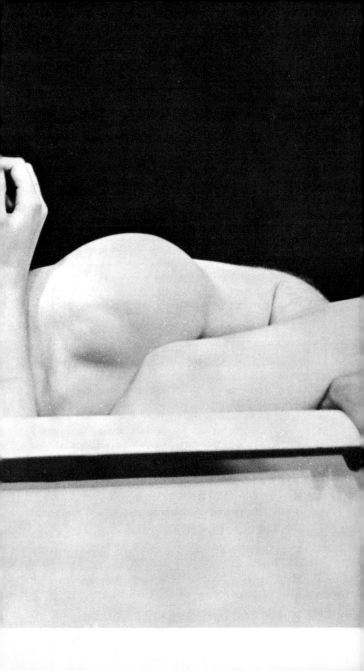

MAN: That's great, but what do we do after we take a bath?

WOMAN: I don't know. How would I know that?

MAN: Well, I know what I want to do.

WOMAN: Fine, but I don't. Except that I want to take a bath.

MAN: Listen, it's after five o'clock!

WOMAN: O.K. I mean, if you feel like you want to leave, I'll understand. You know, we'll run into each other at Jimmie's again, or you can give me a call if you want to. Whatever you want to do is all right with me. (*She gets up, goes to the hall, lights the light, starts water running in the bathtub.*)

MAN: Hey! What kind of bullshit is this?

WOMAN (*From the hallway*): What are you getting so uptight about?

MAN: Uptight?! You're the one who's uptight.

WOMAN: No, man. I just want to take a bath. I'm dirty, not uptight. (*She goes into the bedroom, puts on light. She is humming while she strips. Throws clothes on floor, picks up an old satin robe from the bed, puts it on.*)

MAN (*rises, yelling into bedroom*): Listen, I think I'm gonna go.

WOMAN (*from bedroom*): Will I see you?

MAN: I doubt it.

WOMAN: Why, what's the matter? (*She comes back in from bedroom, stands facing him across the room.*) Hey, what's bugging you? All I did was ask if you wanted to take a bath with me.

MAN: And what am I supposed to do? Say "Yes, ma'am" and hop into the tub like a nice boy?

WOMAN: If you want to.

MAN: And then what? Supposing you decide you don't want to go to bed with me.

WOMAN: So?

MAN: So what am I supposed to do, jerk off? Walk around with my balls clanging together?

WOMAN: Oh, that's it—you're afraid you're going to get all hot and you won't come. Is that it?

MAN (*a little embarrassed, then*): Yeah, I . . . I guess so. I suppose that's it. I mean, is that so fucking unusual?

WOMAN: No, no of course not. Why didn't you just say that instead of getting so upset?

Pause. He looks incredulously at her. She smiles benignly.

Well, all right, don't worry about that. I'll guarantee that you won't have to leave here without coming. O.K.?

He is scratching his head.

Don't worry about it. You'll come. Now, you want to take a nice, warm bath?

MAN (*shrugs his shoulders, gives in*): Oh, well. Why not. (*Mostly to himself.*) Some operator I turned out to be.

She has turned to go to the bathtub. He is following. They get to the tub, he looks around, she turns off water and tests it with her hand.

WOMAN: Groovy.

MAN: You got a john in here?

She points, and he goes into john, puts the light on. The walls are covered with photographs of nude men and women, a collage of art shots, nudist magazine stuff, porno shots. He closes the door.

MAN: Jesus Christ!

WOMAN: What is it?

MAN: Nothing. It was just the wallpaper. Took me a little by surprise.

WOMAN: Great, isn't it? I hardly ever notice it anymore. It was something I did a couple of years ago—you know, one of those projects on a rainy Sunday.

MAN: Some people read *The Times*.

He has his back to audience, facing the toilet. He is pissing. We hear the sound of the water. She is now in the tub.

WOMAN: Hey, you ought to get in here. It feels wonderful.

161

He comes out of the john, strips, joins her in the tub. It's all very awkward, but they wind up facing each other, each leaning against one end of the tub, legs in the middle.

Isn't it wonderful?

MAN: Yes it is, I have to admit it—it's great. Listen, don't get me wrong. I don't have anything against this kind of thing.

She smiles at him. He smiles too, relaxing.

WOMAN: I like you, you know? You're really a nice guy.

MAN: I like you too.

He leans forward to kiss her. She leans forward too. With some strain they reach each other's lips. She has a sponge in her hand and starts to wash his back.

WOMAN: Good?

MAN: Great.

He starts to inch forward in his sitting position, trying to get her legs up over his shoulders, wanting to make genital contact.

WOMAN: Hey, why don't you just relax? That's a pretty uncomfortable way of doing things. (*She looks down at his crotch. Sweetly, as to a child:*) Oh, just look at you. You're all hard and big. (*She starts to play with his penis, massaging and soaping it. We cannot see that, of course, because of the side of the tub.*) Mmmmmmm. I just love penises. I think they're so cute.

He sits back, relaxes, enjoying.

MAN: Oh, this is the life.

She continues to play with him, and he is getting hotter and hotter. Suddenly, he pulls away, back from her.

O.K., hold it. Wait a minute.

WOMAN: What's the matter?

MAN: Well, I don't really want to come this way.

WOMAN: No?

MAN: Well, no.

WOMAN: Does it make any difference to you which way you come?

MAN: Sure it makes a difference.

WOMAN: Oh. Well, don't come then.

MAN: Oh, sure. Listen, I'm not Mr. Self-Control you know.

WOMAN: I thought you just wanted to make sure you'd come. I didn't think it made any difference how you came.

MAN: Well, it's just that I . . . I mean, I'd like to come inside you.

Lights are dimming.

WOMAN: O.K., that's cool. Let's get out of the tub and I'll dry you off and powder you so you'll feel really beautiful and then we can get into bed.

MAN: Now you're talking business.

Blackout

Lights up. He is lying in bed, on his back, so we see the top of his head. She is standing at the foot of the bed, brushing out her hair.

Oh, man, I feel great.

WOMAN: Me too.

He reaches over and examines a whole variety of stuff on the table next to bed.

MAN: Jesus, you're really prepared.

WOMAN: Sure. You wouldn't cook without spices, would you?

MAN: Amies, grass, body lotion. What's this, a vibrator?

WOMAN (*matter-of-factly*): Mm-hmm. Whatever—you know?

MAN: Sure.

WOMAN (*finished with her hair*): Hey, you like tõ use a mirror?

MAN: Well, I usually don't bother with any of that, but it's up to you.

WOMAN: Groovy.

She crosses room. Against the wall is an enormous wood-framed mirror attached to a rolling stand. She brings it over to the foot of the bed, tilts it. Now we can see him lying on the bed through the mirror.

Is that all right? Can you see?

MAN: Fine. Perfect.

She gets on the foot of the bed. He stretches his arms high in the air, reaches back, and takes hold of the brass headboard.

You've got a great body, you know?

WOMAN: Yes, I know. It sure turns a lot of people on, so I guess it's O.K.

MAN: You know? I've never really met anybody like you.

WOMAN: Oh, that's nice.

Now she crouches between his legs, kneeling there, facing him. Through the mirror we can see her back and his genitals are covered by it. She starts to kiss his legs, his chest, thighs, and so on. Then, although we cannot see it, it should be obvious that she is going down on him. Her body, still in the kneeling position between his legs, is undulating. He is getting closer and closer to an orgasm.

MAN (*through gritted teeth*): Wait, wait, let me fuck you.

She shakes her head and makes a sound as if to say no.

Come on, I really want to put it inside of you.

Again she indicates no.

Come on. Look, I really want to.

Again no. He is a little annoyed, getting angry, agressive. Finally, he reaches down, pulls her off him. She is struggling, but he gets her down on her back—so that she is in the position he was in—and he mounts her. Of course, through the mirror we see only his body on top of her. She goes limp, turns off.

WOMAN (*turned off, annoyed*): Oh Christ, go ahead if you have to. Damn!

He groans, finishes coming, then sags on top of her. She strokes him indulgently. Silence for a moment.

Didn't you like what I was doing? I mean, why'd you stop me?

MAN (*he bolts upright, moves off her, sits facing her*): What the fuck is the matter with you?! Why does it have to be your way? Always your way?

WOMAN: You get so uptight, for no reason at all.

MAN: No reason? That's a laugh.

WOMAN: Weren't you having a good time when I was going down on you?

MAN: Of course I was.

WOMAN: Well, so was I.

MAN: But I told you, I wanted to come inside you.

WOMAN: Well, my mouth is inside me. What's wrong with that?

MAN: There's nothing wrong with that.

WOMAN: I was into a whole thing of worshipping your cock. You know, really making love to it, and it was groovy, and you liked it too. I don't understand.

He is incredulous.

First you wanted a guarantee you would come. Then you have a whole special thing about where you want to come. Can't you just relax and have a good time? I mean, what makes you think I'm lookin' to do you in? You think I get kicks out of that?

MAN: Man, you're really blowin' my mind! (*He falls down on the bed on his back, next to her.*) I don't know whether I'm crazy or you're crazy.

WOMAN: Look, I never met a man I couldn't make it with if I wanted to. You just get nervous for nothing.

MAN: I think somebody sent you here to get me, that's what I think. I feel weird.

WOMAN: Well, look. What do you say we just turn over and get some sleep. O.K.?

He is silent, staring up at the ceiling. She shrugs, gives him a little peck on the cheek, gets under the covers and turns her back to him, closes her eyes, heading for sleep.

Good night.

He is silent, staring. The lights slowly fade to black.

END

The Empress' New Clothes

The commentary is shared by two men. Choreography supplies visual aids, illustrating the garments described by the commentators. Song:

  Knickers, knickers—
  Those are the things to have,
  You puts them on in the bedroom,
  You takes them off in the lav . . .

  Knickers, knickers,
  Those are the things to wear,
  For if you buy a nice pair of knickers,
  Then you won't have your bum all bare . . .

COMMENTATOR 1: The lyrics are by John Osborne, from his play "Under Plain Cover," presented at the Royal Court Theatre, London, in 1962.

COMMENTATOR 2:
  The vision of knickers that thou dost see
  Is my vision's greatest enemy.

COMMENTATOR 1: Visions of knickers have traditionally haunted the English imagination. Not visions of cami-knickers . . .

Projection of cami-knickers.

Nor visions of panties, formerly known as "step-ins" . . .

Projection of panties.

169

Nor visions of girdles, which are to the bottom what Stalinism is to Communism—

Projection of panty-girdle.

Nor—God forbid—visions of nylon briefs . . .

Projection of nylon briefs.

But visions of knickers in all their classic forms.

COMMENTATOR 2: "If Victorian dress was a monument to Victorian morals, this humble garment formed, as it were, the keystone of the arch."

COMMENTATOR 1: Said the late C. Willett Cunnington, famous historian of English underwear.

COMMENTATOR 2: Let us go back to the origins of knickers. You may think they are lost in antiquity.

COMMENTATOR 1: If so, you are wrong.

COMMENTATOR 2: You may also assume that the history of knickers from Queen Victoria's day to our own would show a steady development from armor-plated Puritanism towards wide-open permissiveness.

COMMENTATOR 1: Wrong again.

Group of girls appears, dressed in 1800 style.

COMMENTATOR 2: The time is 1800. Here is a group of young ladies about whom Jane Austen might have written. Not one of them is wearing knickers. Skirts, petticoats, underskirts—yes. But no knickers.

COMMENTATOR 1: Knickers—or drawers, as they were originally called—were unknown in England during this period. We sometimes laugh at the elaborate formality that governed the relationship between the sexes. In fact, it was a highly exciting game. Given a chance encounter in a dark corridor and good will on both sides, seduction could take place in a matter of seconds.

COMMENTATOR 2: Meanwhile, in France, knickers were worn only by women of loose morals. A Parisian journalist wrote: "Except for actresses, Parisian ladies never wear drawers."

Projected caption appears: "KNICKERS—1800-1820."

COMMENTATOR 1: This was a great era of accidental

revelations. Thomas Rowlandson showed one of them in a celebrated print—"Taking a Five-Barred Gate—Flying!"

Projection of print.

COMMENTATOR 2: But as the Industrial Revolution gathered momentum, the textile manufacturers, greedy for profits, put a new garment on the market —pantaloons, otherwise known as pantalets. They came down to the ankle, where they were trimmed with lace or muslin. Naturally, only the lower part of the garment was visible.

Projection of lower part of skirt, revealing edge of pantalets.

COMMENTATOR 1: A few audacious young aristocrats began to adopt the new fashion. One of them was Princess Charlotte, daughter of George IV. Once, after dinner with Lady De Clifford, she stretched out her legs and shocked her hostess.

LADY DE CLIFFORD: My dear Princess Charlotte, you show your drawers.

PRINCESS CHARLOTTE: I never do, but where I can put myself at ease.

LADY DE CLIFFORD: Yes, my dear, but when you get in or out of a carriage . . .

PRINCESS CHARLOTTE: I don't care if I *do* show them. The Duchess of Bedford's are much longer—and they are bordered with Brussels lace.

LADY DE CLIFFORD: If she must wear them, she does right to make them handsome. But to make them not only handsome but *visible*—that is beyond forgiveness.

COMMENTATOR 1: Pantalets were rare—and even on the legs of a princess they were considered highly immodest, if not depraved.

COMMENTATOR 2: And they were hardly ever what they seemed to be. We get our image of pantalets from Broadway and Hollywood.

Projection of movie still from "G.W.T.W." or "Seven

*Brides"; or live girl raising skirt to reveal traditional
image of pantalets.*

It is blatantly inaccurate. For the most part, pantalets consisted of a pair of separate tubes, tied at the knees. They were worn mainly by schoolgirls, who used them to protect their stockings on muddy country walks.

*Live girl raises skirt to reveal pantalets as described
with bare thighs above.*

COMMENTATOR 1: We have reached 1820. There is still no sign of knickers—in the sense of pants that start at the hip and end just under the knee.

Projected caption appears: "KNICKERS—1820-1840."

COMMENTATOR 2: A woman born in 1812 writes as follows:

LADY'S VOICE: No girl that I knew wore drawers—nothing but leggings tied below the knee—till about 1830.

COMMENTATOR 2: Even then, the new fashion was strictly confined to the upper classes. The lady continues:

LADY'S VOICE: They were not worn at all by common people. Such people in those days did not imitate gentry. There were three classes then. Now the poorest think they may imitate their betters.

COMMENTATOR 2: It was felt that drawers were unhealthy and indecent—and that it was an outrage to dress girls up like boys.

COMMENTATOR 1: 1837—Queen Victoria is crowned—

Projection of Victoria's coronation.

—almost certainly wearing no knickers. It is possible that she did not don her first pair of knickers until after the death of her consort, Prince Albert, in 1861.

COMMENTATOR 2: Recognizable knickers first began to creep into use during the 1830's and then only among the sophisticates. They consisted of two long tubes of material attached to a waistband.

Girls model them.

It's crucial to remember that they had no crotch.

Girls demonstrate the lack of crotch. Projected caption appears: "KNICKERS—1840-1860."

COMMENTATOR 1: 1840—drawers are colloquially known as "sit-down-upons."

COMMENTATOR 2: 1841—"sit-upons."

COMMENTATOR 1: 1843—"unutterables"—a clear indication that they were entering the private vocabulary of public people.

COMMENTATOR 2: 1850—Lady Chesterfield writes a letter to her daughter. In it she refers to:

LADY CHESTERFIELD: —those comfortable garments which we have borrowed from the other sex, and which all of us wear but none of us talk about.

COMMENTATOR 1: In 1855, the British Ambassador in Paris made a report on the state visit of the King of Italy.

AMBASSADOR (*writing*): At a state reception, a lady-in-waiting had the misfortune to trip over her crinoline skirt and tumble head-long in full view of the Imperial party. Whereupon the King exclaimed with enthusiasm to the Empress: "I am delighted to see, Madame, that your ladies do not wear drawers, and that the gates of paradise are always open."

As he speaks girl in crinoline trips and somersaults.

COMMENTATOR 1: Soon afterwards, the King visited Windsor Castle, where Queen Victoria found his conversation "startling in the extreme." She decorated him with the Order of the Garter.

COMMENTATOR 2: 1859—extract from a letter written by the Hon. Eleanor Stanley, lady-in-waiting to Queen Victoria.

LADY'S VOICE: I hear the latest new "fast" ladies' fashion is said to be wearing "knickerbockers."

As she speaks, girl in crinoline trips and somersaults.

COMMENTATOR 1: The Duchess of Manchester, getting too hastily over a stile, caught a hoop of her cage in it and went regularly head over heels. They say there was never such a thing seen—and the other ladies hardly knew whether to be thankful or not that a part of her underclothing consisted in a pair of scarlet tartan knickerbockers—which were revealed to the view of all the world in general and the Duc de Malakoff in particular. Enigmatically, he remarked later:

DUC DE MALAKOFF: Ma chère, c'est diabolique!

COMMENTATOR 1: Looking back on the middle years of the nineteenth century, a woman wrote to *The Girl's Own Paper* about the pioneer epoch of knickers:

COMMENTATOR 2: "For a long time, if anybody dared dream of such an innovation, she dared not speak of it—and when at last the bounds were leaped by some courageous woman who donned the first drawers, there was a wonderful hue and cry . . . Women wear garments like men! Women trying to get into trousers! Horror! Shame!"

COMMENTATOR 1: Why the horror? Why the shame? Public opinion now began to be heard, and the simple, overwhelming argument against knickers was that they were indecent and un-Christian.

CLERGYMAN *with Welsh accent appears in pulpit.*

CLERGYMAN: My text today is Deuteronomy, Chapter 22, Verse 5: "The woman shall not wear that which pertaineth unto a man, neither shall a man put on a woman's garment; for all that do so are abomination unto the Lord thy God." The word of the Lord is plain for all to comprehend. If there be any woman in this congregation today who is wearing garments pertaining unto a man—in short, who is wearing drawers—let me warn her that she is an abomination unto the Lord her God. If she would enter into the Kingdom of Heaven, let her cast off this diabolical raiment, which is nothing more nor less than a device of the Devil.

COMMENTATOR 2: Families of the period were divided on the subject—as deeply divided as the garments themselves.

MIDDLE-CLASS MOTHER: Sarah, my dear child—you cannot complain that your father and I have been tyran-

175

nous in your upbringing. Is there nothing we can do
to persuade you that the course you have chosen is
the Devil's way?

DAUGHTER: Nothing, Mamma. My life belongs to the
future and I must trust my own judgment. I know you
think me sinful. Nevertheless I am determined to
wear drawers.

Projected caption: "KNICKERS—1860-1880."

COMMENTATOR 1: These were two decades that trans-
formed the social distribution and physical design of
knickers. During the 1860's they spread from the
aristocracy to the middle classes—though they remained, as always, split between the legs.

LADY'S VOICE: I was wearing the usual feminine drawers
that are open behind.

COMMENTATOR 1: Says the tormented heroine of "The
Memoirs of Dolly Morton," a famous erotic novel

dealing with the Civil War. The author of "Rose Fielding"—another pornographic classic of the period—contains an even more explicit description.

AUTHOR: Women's pants are made, to speak plainly, with openings at the front and rear, corresponding to her natural openings . . . The garments are no obstruction whatever to a man who is determined to violate a woman.

Projection of open drawers.

COMMENTATOR 1: Not everyone felt unobstructed. The anonymous author of "My Secret Life"—the erotic autobiography of a Victorian lecher—takes another point of view.

2ND AUTHOR: More and more this fashion of wearing drawers seems to be spreading. Formerly, no woman wore them, but now—whether lady, servant or whore—they all wear them. I find they hinder those comfortable chance feels of bum and cunt of which I have had so many.

COMMENTATOR 2: Despite opposition from prudes and lechers, who found themselves for once on the same side, knickers were sold in increasing numbers throughout the 1860's.

COMMENTATOR 1: They remained open-crotched until the revolutionary innovation of 1876. That was the year in which "closed drawers" appeared for the first time.

Projection of closed drawers.

Before 1876, the lines of battle were easily defined—between those who wore knickers and those who didn't. After 1876, the area of conflict grew smaller. Apart from the working class—who still wore nothing—there were those who wore "open drawers"—

Projection of open drawers.

and those who preferred them closed.

Projected caption: "KNICKERS—1880-1900."

COMMENTATOR 2: The debate raged for many years. A prominent advocate of open drawers was Frank

Harris, editor of *The Saturday Review* and author of "My Life and Loves."

HARRIS: I withdrew my hand and rebuked her. "You have closed drawers, you cheat," I said, and I urged her to wear the other sort of drawers. I told her how I had suggested to a friend of mine, who was a photographer, that he should make two contrasting pictures. One of a girl wearing open drawers, entitled "Free Trade"; and the other of a girl wearing closed ones, entitled "Protection." He sold over a million postcards in a month, and gave me a thousand pounds for the idea. Now, as always, I am an impenitent advocate of Free Trade.

Projected caption: "KNICKERS—1880-1914."

COMMENTATOR 1: 1881—the word "knickers," derived from the masculine "knickerbockers," is used for the first time in England.

COMMENTATOR 2: Knickers at last reach the working classes. There is a vast blossoming of knickers in the advertisement columns of magazines and newspapers.

COMMENTATOR 1: Nainsook knickers with frills of muslin embroidery, 5/6d.

COMMENTATOR 2: French drawers of washing silk, threaded with baby ribbon, for those who like a froth of frillies.

COMMENTATOR 1: Close-fitting Directoire knickers which the up-to-date maiden delights in.

COMMENTATOR 2: Fine stockinette *culottes* with ribbon bow at the knee and elastic at knee and waist, 3/3d.

COMMENTATOR 1: C. Willett Cunnington sagely comments:

COMMENTATOR 2: "The theft of masculine garments has always been considered at first fast, then fashionable, and finally common."

COMMENTATOR 1: But the stage remained conservative. A new dance reasserted the old tradition—CAN-CAN.

A girl enters in Can-Can costume, places herself back to audience and bends over, raising her skirt. She is knickerless.

COMMENTATOR 2: Pronounced "Con-Con."

COMMENTATOR 1: Proof that knickers were at last being worn by the proletariat is supplied by many music-hall songs of the 1890's. The following lyric obviously refers to a pair of open knickers:

GIRL SINGER:
> Chase me, Charlie, chase me, Charlie,
> I've lost the leg of my drawers!
> Chase me, Charlie, chase me, Charlie,
> Won't you lend me yours?

COMMENTATOR 1: Nobody wearing closed knickers could possibly lose a single leg. Toward the end of the century, the bicycle boom began.

GIRL SINGER:
> Some folks think bicycling a thing
> A girl should not go in for:
> But their idea of fun, for one,
> I do not care a pin for.
> So if your figure's trim and slim,
> Put on your knickerbockers,
> And shut your eyes to cheers and jeers
> From rude street-arab mockers . . .
>
> My eye! Here's a lady bicyclist!
> Look at her! Look at her! Look at her!
>   Look at her!
> Hi! Hi! Hi!
> She's put her petticoat up the spout,
> And now she has to go without:
> She hopes her mother won't find out,
> And thinks she won't be missed.
> Oh, my! Hi, hi!
> Keep your eye on the lady bi-
> The lady bicyclist!

COMMENTATOR 2: But open knickers gallantly survived, even into the new century. American ads of the period refer to "Ladies' Closed Drawers" and "Ladies' Tights, with Closed Seat." Why so much emphasis on the fact that they were closed, unless open ones were also available?

COMMENTATOR 1: Here—to quote John Osborne again —"we come to the flower of the form, believed by most to be decadent. They have long legs, never more than about four inches above the knee, which makes sitting down, getting out of cars, riding bicycles, or going upstairs in buses a tremendous adventure. They always—repeat always—have elastic top and bottom. What the flying buttress was to Gothic, so is elastic top and bottom to Classical Perpendicular or Directoire style. And it is only in knickers that one is still able to find that strange repository of mystery—the gusset."

A girl bends over to reveal the gusset.

COMMENTATOR 2: "Ah—the gusset—I wonder what the chap Betjeman would say about all this."

COMMENTATOR 1: "Nowadays they are mostly worn by elderly or very square middle-aged ladies, and can still be bought in fast decreasing numbers from places like Debenham and Freebody, although High Street, Kensington, still remains the richest field, with Derry and Toms and, above all, Pontings, stubbornly carrying on the old tradition. I suppose one might almost say that the end of knickers came with the rise of nylon."

COMMENTATOR 2: "True. It was nylon really killed them."

COMMENTATOR 1: "They were never quite the same afterwards. The heavy whisper of descending pink silk was soon to be heard in the land no more. All was hard-faced, unembarrassed, unwelcoming nylon."

Projected caption: "KNICKERS SINCE 1914."

COMMENTATOR 2: By the time World War One broke out, open knickers were extinct and the classic period was over.

COMMENTATOR 1: In the 1920's came the Windsor Washanredy Krinkle Krepe Bloomers and the Step-In Shorty Bloomers.

COMMENTATOR 2: The 1930's produced Kickaway Panties . . .

COMMENTATOR 1: Skin-Light Skin-Tight Briefs . . .

MODEL 1: They fit without a wrinkle!

COMMENTATOR 1: Ginger Rogers Lace Panties . . .

MODEL 2: Ginger chose this clever little panty for herself!

COMMENTATOR 1: And the Famous Four-in-One panty, brassiere, girdle, and vest . . .

MODEL 3: As worn by Miss Loretta Young.

COMMENTATOR 1: But the magic had fled. Knickers in their classic form . . .

COMMENTATOR 2: Hip-gripping and open-crotched . . .

COMMENTATOR 1: Confining yet exposing . . .

COMMENTATOR 2: Had vanished. Instead, we have all-concealing knicker-substitutes . . .

COMMENTATOR 1: More rigidly Puritanical than any other kind of underwear in human history.

Both sigh in unison.

COMMENTATOR 2: We haven't moved from Victorian prudery to modern liberty.

COMMENTATOR 1: We have moved from a time of moral prohibition and easy physical access . . .

COMMENTATOR 2: To a time of moral relaxation and physical invulnerability.

COMMENTATOR 1: In 1800, they wore no knickers and read the Bible.

COMMENTATOR 2: Today they wear body-stockings and read "Portnoy's Complaint."

Music has started to creep in since the sigh—a choral humming of the Osborne tune with which the sketch began. It now bursts out into a nostalgic reprise of Osborne's lyric:

CHORUS:

Knickers, knickers
Those are the things to wear;
For if you buy a nice pair of knickers,
Then you won't have your bum all bare.

Sung with full sentimental rallentando.

BLACKOUT

ꞓ Love is a Merry, Splendid Thing

At rise: Vietnam. Night just on the outskirts of the jungle. A cut-away of a Vietnamese peasant's hut. A young Vietnamese wife sits up late and alone, rocking her baby. Suddenly, a sound in the jungle . . . A sound that is decidedly different from the "nice" jungle sounds we have been hearing . . . Sounds of soft twittering and Asian woodblocks . . . No, this sound is decidedly different, for it is the unmistakable sound of a bullshit birdcall. She jumps at the sound. She smiles. The sound is repeated.

THE WIFE: It is your father, little one.

She runs outside the hut to call back into the jungle with "the pre-arranged all cool birdcall." It is even dumber than the original one, but it works: Enter: LT. VAN TRAN TAN of the N.L.F. He's fucking gorgeous! . . . They rush to each other and embrace . . . It is a Neo-Stalinist art poster . . . They break the embrace and he pulls out a bomber of a joint from his rucksack.

THE WIFE: Oh, wow . . . you brought a joint.

THE HUSBAND: I brought *two* joints. This second one is laced with a little hash . . . for later.

THE WIFE: And how goes our war of liberation, my brave husband?

THE HUSBAND: Well, I took these two joints off a captured American Full Bird Colonel . . . so *you* tell *me*

185

how the war is going. (*Looks down at his little son.*)
Oh, wow . . . little Van looks outasight!

THE WIFE: Come . . . come inside, my husband . . .
The Green Berets have been watching this village.

*They go inside happily, arm-in-arm. She goes into
some fast cooking numbers and he plays with the kid
and lights up one of the joints and they smile at each
other and pass the joint back and forth and pass
kisses back and forth and he smacks her on her fine
ass and roams around his own pad happily, stopping
only long enough to straighten up a poster on the
wall . . . a huge poster of Joan Baez. Then, being too
horny to wait for food, he pulls her out of the cooking mode and grabs for her.*

THE WIFE: I love you so.
THE HUSBAND: And I love you.
THE WIFE: Do you love me? Say you love me.
THE HUSBAND: I just said it.
THE WIFE: Say it again . . . no . . . *prove it* . . . seduce
me . . . I lie here all alone at night dreaming of how
you used to seduce me . . . seduce me, Van . . . *take*
me.

*He starts slow . . . her neck and a little shoulder
action . . . a few items of clothing dropped to the
floor . . . onto a crude bed or mat . . . onto the deck
. . . he begins to get into it . . . he starts wailing . . .
it is soon clear he is going to lay a great fuck on her
in honor of the departed French who once taught in
that country. Down he goes on her teats . . . taking
off the rest of her clothes at the same time and some
of his own . . . she is starting to get a little vocal as
she gets more and more into it all . . . now all clothes
are off . . . He takes on her navel—but she can wait
no longer and her hands fly down to guide his head
to her snatch. She lets out a long, great sigh and says
plaintively:*

THE WIFE: Ohhh . . . yesssss . . . yesssss . . . yes!

*It must be noted here that this chick is one of those
chicks who talks a great deal while being eaten. In*

*her case the word "Yes" is the favorite word . . .
although "ahhhh" is in some favor.*

Enter from the jungle: Two GREEN BERETS *with M-16
rifles. They crash out of the jungle loudly enough to
be heard by* THE HUSBAND *and* THE WIFE. *The two*
GREEN BERETS *see the hut and with head signals and
elaborate hand signals they advance toward it.* THE
HUSBAND *is in a bit of a panic. He knows that he is a
soldier and a revolutionary first and a great blow job
second. Americans' combat boots are crunching
loudly and steadily toward the hut.* THE HUSBAND
starts to get up.

THE WIFE: Oh no . . . don't stop . . . don't ever stop.

THE HUSBAND: . . . well . . . yeah, but . . . like . . .

1ST GREEN BERET (*under his breath to the other*): Take
two and cut to the right . . . got it?

The other beret nods yes.

Now!

*They charge the hut . . . crash through a wall . . .
The hut caves in . . . confusion . . . chaos . . . a baby
cries . . . voices . . . curses . . . They drown* THE
WIFE *in a plethora of well-meant apologies and right
the hut as best they can and when order is somewhat
restored we see that* THE WIFE *is still on her back
bare-assed and hot to trot, but she has wisely covered
her husband's body with a tarp or blanket or something . . . at any rate . . . he is still down there somewhere.*

1ST BERET (*picking up the baby and putting it back in
its cradle*): Aw hey . . . sorry about that, little fella.
(*To* 2ND BERET:) He's a cute little fella . . . reminds me of my own kid . . . except for the deformed
eyes, you know.

2ND BERET (*to* THE WIFE): Oh . . . evening ma'am . . .
sorry we had to disturb you like that, but we have to
watch our steps in these little out-of-the-way places.

THE WIFE: Yes, I'll bet you do.

With a sweet smile to the two BERETS *she takes her
hands, which up until now have been outside this*

blanket/tent arrangement, and slowly, innocently, slips them underneath, and we see some sort of vague movement which leads us to believe she is suggesting that her HUSBAND *continue with his earlier mission . . . indeed . . . She soon begins to relate to it . . . while at the same time keeping in mind the presence of The Enemy.*

1ST BERET: See, actually, ma'am . . . we're sort of canvassing the neighborhood, taking a minute or two out to talk to all the wives and mothers in the area . . .

THE WIFE (*abstract*): . . . yes . . . oh, yes . . . yes . . .

The 2ND BERET *moves in with his buddy and the two of them take out training aids and pamphlets from their pockets.*

2ND BERET: We like to call it our little "Pacification Program" . . . you get it?

THE WIFE: . . . yes . . . oh . . . oh yes . . . ohhh yes . . . yes

1ST BERET (*really encouraged by this response*): Say, you sure are easy to talk to. She's great to talk to, isn't she?

2ND BERET: She sure is. I'll be honest with you ma'am . . . a lot of the girls in this neighborhood are . . . well . . .

1ST BERET: A little uptight . . .

2ND BERET: And it's probably because their men folk are gone.

1ST BERET: Right. And we know *why* they're gone . . .

2ND BERET: And what they're doing . . .

1ST BERET: And to be quite honest about it, ma'am . . . we happen to know that your husband is one of them.

THE WIFE: Oh . . . yes . . . yes . . . yesssssssss. . . .

1ST BERET (*a little shaken*): . . . oh . . . so you *admit* it?

THE WIFE (*shutting her eyes*): . . . yes, darling . . . yes . . . yes . . .

2ND BERET: Well, dammit . . . good for you.

A pause while they check their pamphlets and turn pages and check notes, etc.

THE WIFE: Oh, don't stop . . . don't stop . . . please don't stop.

1ST BERET: Just checkin' our notes here . . . want to make sure we present all this just right . . .

THE WIFE: Oh, that's so wonderful.

1ST BERET (*on top of it again*): You see . . . it's up to you girls. When the men sneak back to the villages at night . . . talk to them . . . tell them how much you and the kids miss them . . . tell them the Americans are good guys and gave the kids candy . . .

2ND BERET: And tell him what he's doing is *wrong* . . . and he should stop it and till his fields instead.

THE HUSBAND *has obviously been doing a great job down there because* THE WIFE *looks like she's on the verge of an orgasm.*

THE WIFE: Oh . . . oh . . . yes . . . yes . . . yes . . .

1ST BERET (*going into their big finish*): And remember ma'am . . . if *your* country goes down . . . then Laos will go down . . . and Thailand . . .

THE WIFE (*it's starting to happen now*): Oh . . . oh . . . yesss . . . yessss . . . yesssss . . . ?????

2ND BERET: And then Cambodia will go down . . .

THE WIFE: . . . yes . . .

1ST BERET: And even Burma could go down.

THE WIFE (*the pace quickens*): . . . yes . . . yes . . . yes . . . yes . . . ahhhhhhhh . . . ?????

1ST BERET: Well, you sure seem excited about the theory.

2ND BERET (*shows her a page in his pamphlet*): It's called "The Domino Theory" . . .

THE WIFE (*she is THERE*): . . . ahhh . . . yessss, sssssssssockittome, baby!!

1ST BERET (*glad she likes it*): It's a swell theory, isn't it?

THE WIFE (*moaning softly*): oh yes . . . oh yes . . . so wonderful . . .

2ND BERET: And it was thought out by Dean Rusk . . .

THE WIFE (*obviously heading into number two*): . . . oh . . . oh . . . oh . . . yes . . . yes . . . yes . . . YES . . . ?????

1ST BERET: You maybe didn't hear about him . . . but he was Secretary of State for Lyndon B. Johnson.

THE WIFE (*that does it—she comes all over again . . . the big one*): . . . ahhhh . . . ahhhhhhh . . . you did it again . . .

2ND BERET: Well—we'll be off now ma'am.

1ST BERET: See you, ma'am . . .

They start out, stopping by the crib.

He's a cute little fella . . . bet he's gonna grow up to be just like his Daddy.

They go and vanish in the jungle. A silence. The jungle sounds begin again.

The tarp or blankets are removed by THE HUSBAND, *who rises slowly and falls on top of* THE WIFE.

They kiss. He mounts her slowly, deliberately. The jungle sounds become sweet and musical.

Lights fade slowly.

THE END

1. Leon Russom
2. Margo Sappington
3. Bill Macy

4. Boni Enten
5. George Welbes
6. Katie Drew-Wilkinson
7. Nancy Tribush
8. Alan Rachins
9. Raina Barrett
10. Mark Dempsey